The American Golfer's
Guide to Ireland

The American Golfer's
Guide to Ireland

*Nurturing Your Golfing Soul While
Enjoying an Incomparable Irish Experience*

Bill Ruskin *with* Brian Keogh

authorHOUSE®

AuthorHouse™
1663 Liberty Drive
Bloomington, IN 47403
www.authorhouse.com
Phone: 1-800-839-8640

First published by AuthorHouse   09/24/2011

ISBN: 978-1-4634-4533-1 (sc)

Printed in the United States of America

Edited and augmented by Paul B. W. Miller, PhD, CPA
University of Colorado, Colorado Springs

Cover photo by Larry Lambrecht, L.C. Photography
www.golfstock.net

The par 4 fifth hole at Doonbeg is characteristic of so many others in Ireland with its breathtaking beauty and challenging architecture. Once you manage to look away from the view and down at your ball, you get to decide whether you're going to follow it through a valley directly toward the Atlantic Ocean and the Lodge in the distance by safely laying up off the tee or risk a lost ball in the deep ravine after throwing caution to the wind, which, of course, is always blowing.

CONTENTS

For Brigette

"Once you have found her,
never let her go"

FOREWORD

*C*ONGRATULATIONS! IF YOU'VE *bought this book, the chances are that you will soon be on your way to Ireland for the golfing holiday of a lifetime. Believe me, you are in for an unforgettable experience.*

I've played many of the world's greatest courses but I can honestly say that there is no place like home.

Not only has Ireland got some of the world's best golf courses, it's also one of the most beautiful places on the planet.

Add to that the great welcome you are sure to receive and you will soon be lending this book to friends so they can plan their trips.

Don't forget to stop off on the north coast for a game at great courses such as Castlerock, Portstewart or the Dunluce and Valley courses in Portrush.

I always try to get out for a round when I'm at home in Portrush. If you spot me on the links, don't be afraid to come over and say hello.

Happy golfing,

Graeme McDowell,
US Open Champion, Pebble Beach, 2010

PREFACE

*Golf appeals to the idiot and the child in us. Just how
childlike golfers become is proven by their frequent
inability to count past five.*
-John Updike

EARLIER IN YOUR lifetime, you used to dream you
would play golf in Ireland—now it's going to come
true and nothing will stop you! We have written this guide
to help you live out that dream of playing your favorite game
while you also enjoy the incomparable Irish Experience.

This book is a research tool for the golfer and potential
traveler to the island of Ireland. It provides information
necessary to ensure a successful golf tour by helping you *Go
Prepared!* It offers advice, facts and information you will
need to know to get the most for your time and money. Your
preparation and the knowledge you gain will pay dividends
in greater enjoyment and less stress once you arrive at your
destination.

Make good use of the Internet

If you use this guide along with the Internet, you can
become as knowledgeable as you'd like about golf in Ireland.
Toward that goal, it provides Internet references to not only
many golf courses on the Emerald Island but also refers you

to numerous excellent websites that will be invaluable as you make detailed plans. For example, you can use the Internet to get specific information on golf courses in your itinerary as well as other information on Ireland, such as castles, historic sites, legendary golf clubs, lodging, restaurants, pubs, fishing, genealogy (it seems that most Americans find themselves so much at home in Ireland they begin to hope and then believe they surely have Irish roots somewhere in their ancestry), and many other topics that may be of interest to the golfer and non-golfer alike. This guide and the Internet will make you a *confident and knowledgeable traveler and golfer on the island of Ireland.*

How to capture the Irish Experience

We designed this guide to help you get started planning. For example, you'll find our highly practical "how to" and personal information to be valuable as you set up your itinerary and begin to make arrangements. We encourage using the Internet to make reservations, find tour operators, and learn about the golf courses you'll be playing and check local news sources for dates of festivals and events that should be part of your itinerary.

Unlike other full color and more expensive golf books on Ireland, this guide has no color photographs of golf courses. Instead, we've included an extensive list of websites where you will find plenty of beautiful photos and very detailed information on golf courses in Ireland. Why would we want you to pay for this kind of information when it's free on the Internet?

Learn to play the Irish Way

This book will also help you learn to play golf the Irish Way, which isn't always the same as you might be used to. This sometimes hard-to-swallow truth will become crystal clear when you read Brian's detailed, almost loving advice on playing golf in Ireland.

An important acknowledgement

We extend our sincere appreciation to *Tourism Ireland* and all the staff members who assisted with their services in preparing this guide.

In closing, we thank you for acquiring our book and we hope it proves helpful as you make your plans to play golf and enjoy your total experience while you're on the beautiful green island of Ireland.

Good golfing and safe journey,

Bill Ruskin
billruskin58@gmail.com
(719) 337-2732
Colorado Springs,
Colorado, USA

Brian Keogh
brian.keogh@mac.com
Dublin
The Republic of Ireland

Map of the Island of Ireland

© August 2011 Tourism Ireland

I.

GOLF and the IRISH EXPERIENCE

An Irish Welcome

Here's Céad Míle Fáilte *to friend and to rover,*
That's a greeting that's Irish as Irish can be,
It means you are welcome
A thousand times over,
Wherever you come from,
Whosoever you be.

A Warm Welcome from "Tourism Ireland"

"Maybe the great game of golf wasn't invented in Ireland but to most visitors it certainly seems that way.

"In fact, someone with a lot of time and most likely a low handicap once calculated that there are more golf courses per square mile on the island of Ireland than in any other part of the world. I hope you will have a chance to sample many of them. I can assure you that a golfing visit to Ireland will be the trip of a lifetime for many reasons but especially these four.

---

* *Pronounced Kaid Meela Fawlcha*

1

"*Firstly,* world renowned links courses sparkle like an emerald necklace around the coastline of Ireland. It is subjective and even hazardous to try to pick the best from so many great courses but here are some that are deservedly on golfers' "bucket lists": Royal Portrush, Portstewart. Royal County Down, Baltray, Portmarnock, The European Club, Old Head, Waterville, Ballybunion, Tralee, Lahinch, Doonbeg, Connemara, Carne, Enniscrone, Murvagh, Ballyliffin and Rosapenna.

"*Secondly,* the past two decades have been a remarkable period of developing truly world class golf resorts where the finest facilities and challenging championship level courses will delight guests. They include The K Club, Lough Erne, Druids Glen, Mount Wolsely, Killeen Castle, Glasson, Galgorm Castle, Slieve Russell, The Heritage, Powerscourt, Adare, Fota Island, Dromoland Castle and many more.

"*Thirdly*, visitors will feel more than welcome and helped to enjoy their game at the 400+ private golf clubs scattered generously and invitingly throughout Ireland. Greens fees here offer very good value and the local club members will go out of their way to make you feel at home.

"*Last but not least,* the 19th hole in Ireland is always a great opportunity to meet and swap stories with local golfers eager to share their passion for their favorite sport with visitors. An old saying puts it like this: "There are no strangers in Ireland, only friends you haven't met before."

"Interest in golf in Ireland has increased tremendously in recent years. The 3 Irish Open, Ladies Irish Open, Irish PGA and other high level tournaments attract the world's leading players and receive widespread publicity. It is generally agreed that Ryder Cup 2006 held at the K-Club near Dublin was one of the most fun-filled and successful golfing events ever.

"Irish golfers on the international circuit have also put the spotlight on the great golf to be found on the Island. Padraig Harrington, Graeme McDowell, Rory McIlroy, Darren Clarke, Paul McGinley, Shane Lowrey and others have been both successful and wonderful ambassadors for Irish fun and hospitality.

"I hope you and your friends will experience golf in Ireland for yourselves. I can assure you a warm welcome and wonderful memories."

Joe Byrne
Executive Vice President
Tourism Ireland

Go Prepared: Plan Far Ahead!

Experienced travelers know that if they plan well ahead, they will be more confident and have a more enjoyable tour. If you do that, the Irish will also respect you more because you will know what you are doing. Because you are going to invest considerable time and money to make this dream trip a reality, you will want to use this guide to make that preparation and, above all, to help you enjoy a true *Irish Experience* in addition to great golf. Before you actually start planning the trip, you'll want to absorb the guidance offered by John Hehir, Director of Sales and Marketing at Dromoland Castle. He has a great philosophy that applies especially well to golfers making their first trip to the Emerald Island.

John believes that every American golfer should plan for more than just a golfing trip. The Irish are unpretentious and the desire and goal of the people in the Irish visitor industry is to help Americans enjoy the total *Irish*

Experience—a blending of golf with the social side of Ireland. This combination is born when golfers select from the incredible array of golf courses in the four corners of Ireland and also make an effort to engage with the people they meet through visits to the pubs, in hotels and restaurants, while also taking time to learn about Ireland by attending local festivals and visiting heritage and historical sites.

To avoid frustration and the disappointment of missing a tee time, John believes an important part of the Irish Experience is to decide on the type of courses you will be playing after taking into account that driving times are unique in Ireland and much different (longer) than in the USA. Although Ireland is about the size of the state of Maine geographically, the driving is a total different matter. In other words, do you want to play a mix of links and parkland courses, or will it be all links on this trip? Whatever you decide, be certain you include adequate time to drive to the next course.

One advantage of using an Ireland-based tour company, if you want to consider this arrangement, is their experience and complete understanding of the time it takes to get from one place to another. Thus, they will arrange an itinerary that reflects all factors needed for an enjoyable tour. A good operator will take you off the beaten path, away from places in the popular hit-and-run tourist guidebooks and into the unknown golf courses that are old and authentic. This approach can enhance the whole experience of playing golf in Ireland. If you decide to use a tour company, be certain to select one with Irish personnel. Be cautious about using a tour company (perhaps found on the Internet) that is based in the USA and offers inexpensive golf tours. The Irish tourism industry wants you to leave Ireland with that 'feel good factor' at the end of tour instead of feeling you missed out on too much.

If you've been to Ireland before, you can certainly try to plan your own trip but be sure to arrange (and later confirm) tee times on the golf courses you have chosen to play, select the visitor attractions you would like to see and then allow sufficient driving time to bring your itinerary together.

Many golfers, both professionals and amateurs, have gone before you and experienced Ireland as it should be. For example, Tom Watson has helped bring Irish golf to the forefront by giving credit to practice at Ballybunion for his win at the British Open in the early 80's. Stewart Cink practiced at Doonbeg, Lahinch and Ballybunion to get exposed to the dunes and the wind before he went across to Scotland to win the British Open in 2009. Payne Stewart loved to play golf in Ireland and Tiger Woods and other professionals usually practice on the Irish links before crossing to Scotland for The Open. It's not all business, for it's reported they all love the same Irish experience we're encouraging you to have. Like other enchanted guests in Ireland, they love to walk around and visit pubs and the restaurants, and the Irish folks respect their privacy and treat them as they would the average visitor.

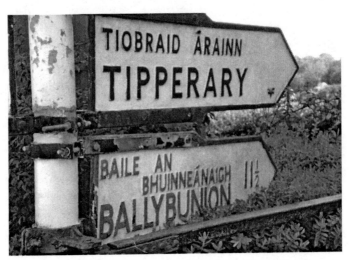

Photo Credit: Bill Ruskin

II.

LET'S GET STARTED—Planning the Golf Tour

"They say golf is life, but don't believe them. Golf is more complicated than that."

Gardner Dickinson

FOR THE READER who doesn't already have an itinerary through an Irish-based or other reliable tour company, we recommend that you begin by assembling your party (a minimum of four is helpful for reserving tee times) and then discussing several key points with your companions. During this discussion, keep in mind that the cost of greens fees is generally fixed, whether you're going deluxe or bargain-basement style. (However, during challenging economic times in 2008-2011, many golf clubs in Ireland offered discounted fees.) As a result, your flexibility in your budget lies with the level of accommodations you prefer and the type of ground transportation you choose. You need to address these basic questions up front:

When to Go

Whenever it is, be certain to plan well ahead of the desired date. A year in advance is a good minimum planning horizon if you want to secure tee times on popular courses. Avoid coming in August if at all possible because it's the busiest time of the year in Europe when the cost of everything can be at a premium and many places are crowded with tourists as well as golfers.

You can count on rain anytime you go to Ireland; but remember that it is not a limiting factor as long as you're prepared for it! The warmest months are May through September. The driest months tend to be March through July and this period is also less busy. May and September are great because golf fees and hotel rates are generally cheaper and the weather tends to be drier.

If you have time and can tear yourself away from the golf course, try to plan your trip to Ireland during one of the many wonderful festivals, or *Fleadhs, (pronounced Flaah)* that occur throughout the country. For example, August brings the *Puck Fair Killorglin* in County Kerry where a goat is crowned King.

If time permits, plan on attending one of the many medieval festivals, banquets or heritage precincts.

A detailed and up-to-the-minute listing of all fairs, festivals and events is available at **www.tourismireland. com**.

Budget for the Tour

In a country where hospitality is second nature, Ireland has a wonderful range of places to stay from the friendliest Bed & Breakfast houses in the world to 5-star hotels. (If you are looking for a bargain and want to take this tour on a very limited budget, then you may find that your ability to plan a successful trip is somewhat constrained. Instead, you may wish to wait another year so that you can save enough money to do the trip as you dreamed it should be.) *On the other hand, if your budget is limited and you're feeling adventurous, you can just go to Ireland on your own, rent a car and drive around and play several of the many great but lesser-known courses. For more information on these spontaneous tours, go to this website* (**www.discoverireland.com**).

To participate in a more structured one-week tour, you should budget airfare ($1,000-1,200), a minimum of $2,500-$3,500 per person for a week's tour, and at least $500 for miscellaneous expenses while in Ireland. As you plan your trip, continually monitor the value of the US dollar against the Euro in Ireland and the British Pound Sterling in Northern Ireland to avoid any surprises upon arrival.

Accommodations

Ireland is full of wonderful Bed & Breakfasts, Country Inns, and Three, Four and Five-Star Hotels. Your choice here will likely have the biggest impact on your total budget. Costs range from $50 to $400 per night per person, depending on the accommodations and the season. For a variety of websites for places to stay, please see the Appendix at the back of this book or again just start your search at **www.discoverireland.com**.

Catherine Treacy, Proprietor of the Killarney Lodge Guesthouse **www.killarneylodge.net** provided us with information that's valuable to both golfers and non-golfers planning a trip to Ireland. Since the housing cost is likely to be your most flexible expense as you set out to plan your tour, a basic understanding of the various types of accommodations available to you is important.

Hotels are given *star* ratings on a scale of 1 to 5 based on various characteristics including service, cleanliness and luxury. A variety of room service charges are associated with hotels. For convenience, they usually have a bar and one or more restaurants.

Guest Houses and Lodges are rated on a scale of 1 to 4. They usually meet most hotel standards but are more family oriented. They usually do not include a restaurant or bar.

Bed and Breakfasts (B&B's) are often private houses, such that you are paying to be a guest in your hosts' home. There are usually no service charges or restaurants or bars in B&B's, so visits to a local pub are in order for food and drink, other than breakfast. The term B&B may be attached to advertising and signs for all categories of accommodation. Keep an eye out for an indication that the B&B offers a "bath *en suite*," which means you'll enjoy a private bathroom.

Other considerations for accommodations

How much you should tip in the various places you visit can be a tough question for travelers. Tipping is expected more in hotels because of the various services provided in the bars and restaurants.

In Guesthouses and B&B's, tipping is optional but always appreciated. A nice tip for a three night stay would be about €10. A couple Euros left on the dresser when you depart is also appropriate. Of course you can always leave a sleeve of new golf balls behind, as they are expensive in Ireland.

Wherever you stay, whether in a small lodging or a large one, make time to meet the owners and the staff as part of the Irish Experience. They are always willing to share information about the area, give accurate directions, and provide travel advice. Don't be afraid to ask for directions; your questions are always answered politely.

Before you decide where to stay, find out if the B&B or Guesthouse you are interested in has an Internet connection and/or wireless service. Also, determine how far your lodging is from town, especially if there is a non-golfer in your party. Most B&B's and Guesthouses are quaint, family owned operations with a personal and "small town" feel. This generally leads to a more enjoyable visit for all parties. In Ireland, golfers are considered special guests in B&B's and Guesthouses and there is great rapport among golfers and proprietors.

As wonderful and cozy as they are, small, family owned B&B's are not always the most suitable accommodations for all golfers, since they may need lots of space, power showers, and larger facilities for drying clothes and relaxing. Because B&B's may be limited in these capacities (after all, you are staying in someone's home which can be very nice) they may be more suited for the traveling couple rather than a group of golfers.

In summary, you can save money by staying in a B&B, as opposed to a Guest House or hotel, but keep in mind that you will likely have a standard room, a double bed, no tub and fewer amenities. There is a good chance you won't have Internet access either.

Renting a home is another approach to accommodation that is gaining popularity among golfers heading for Ireland. See suggested websites in the appendix for details or search the web yourself for a variety of options.

More on Accommodations from Brian Keogh

Visit **www.tourismireland.com** for more information and check out a range of attractive inclusive packages available from many tour operators. As mentioned earlier, Guest Houses, Bed and Breakfasts and self-catering accommodations are classified by a star system from one to four or five stars.

You can choose from many different kinds of hotel or guesthouse, from elegant country homes to luxury castles, village pubs, Georgian manors, budget hotels and Victorian houses. Many four and five star hotels offer a range of food, entertainment, leisure and sporting facilities, including golf courses. You can find welcoming Bed and Breakfasts throughout Ireland, even in the most remote areas, with friendly personal service and wonderful full Irish or Ulster Fry breakfasts.

To feel part of the countryside, nothing compares with a farmhouse vacation, but book early, as they are very popular because it's a great way to get to know local people. Situated in lovely surroundings, Ireland's elegant Country Houses offer truly unique places to stay and often provide access to a variety of pursuits from angling to country cooking courses. As far as possible, book in advance.

Check the Appendix at the back of this book for a complete listing of websites for all types of accommodations in Ireland.

Self-drive or Escorted Tour

Ground transportation costs must also be factored into the budget. The self-drive is the most economical and the most popular, probably because it provides the freedom to roam about on your own. As a result, a wide range of rental vehicles is available. Most are very comfortable, ranging from economical four-passenger cars to nine passenger people mover wagons designed with plenty of space for your gear. (American golfers tend to prefer the Volkswagen Caravelle or Mercedes Vito.) The alternative is an escorted tour, using a large van or small bus, which frees you up from driving, but greatly increases the cost per golfer per day and limits your ability to respond to impulses to explore out of the way places.

TIP: Larger groups (12-16) should consider the bus option. See Chapter XII for detailed information on renting cars and driving in Ireland.

Desired Courses to Play

Ireland has over 400 golf courses but most American golfers are familiar with only a dozen or so. Hundreds of these little known courses are beautiful and challenging and can be played for around €28/£25/$40, with many even less. Popular courses are generally over-subscribed in the summer months and others are very difficult to book, unless you plan well ahead. So, reserve early to play the priority courses.

TIP: Let your Irish-based tour company reserve tee times on the courses you really want to play. For example, they can help you secure a tee time on the desired course for your party, and then design the remainder of the tour around this tee time.

How much golf do you want to play?

As you begin to plan your golf tour, keep in mind the age and physical condition of your companions. Some groups have no problem playing two rounds of golf every day, heading for the pubs in the evening, then falling into bed and starting over the next day. Others play a round a day and do some sightseeing in between. Keep in mind that electric golf carts or "buggies," are not available on many of the courses in Ireland. Depending on your group members' physical condition, design a schedule that won't tire them out so much they can't enjoy the trip. Playing a lot of bad golf on twelve courses may not nurture your soul as much as four to six rounds of good golf. You will enjoy the pilgrimage more if it isn't a marathon!

June has the longest days and you can tee off as late as 7:00 PM. This fact should be taken in consideration as you plan your tour. You may want to play fewer courses or less challenging courses rather than a series of championship courses.

Flights from the USA to Ireland are such that you will likely be worn out by the time you arrive at your hotel, so we recommend that you don't schedule any strenuous golf activity on arrival day. However, a relaxed round with a light supper will ease away those cramps and foggy jet-lagged minds. Be certain that you do *something* on the day you arrive just to keep moving. You'll be tempted to get some sleep, but that will throw your body clock for a loop that can last several days. A relaxed practice round will get you in sync with the local time until you finally make it to your hotel room at the local night hour.

TIP: We can't over emphasize the time it takes to drive between golf courses in Ireland. As a first time golfer to

Ireland, you may want to consider using Shannon as your base especially if you are planning a self-drive tour.

How much does golf cost in Ireland?

When compared to other European destinations (Spain and France, for example), golf in Ireland is a bargain. Old Head has the most expensive greens fees in Ireland at €205 for the regular rate plus €60 for a cart or a similar amount for a caddy. An average caddy cost is €35 plus tip at €20-25 bringing the total cost to the neighborhood of €265/$385 US. The green fee at Royal Portrush ranges from €125/$180 to €140/$200 while Portmarnock can be as low as €40-50/$65-80. All three are championship courses, and you can see how variable the greens fees can be even at that level.

The key is to plan well ahead. Decide where you want to play, check out all desired courses on the Internet, and then begin to arrange your tee times, staying within your budget. One more time, start early because the prime tee times on Ireland's most popular courses can sell out a year in advance for the summer months.

Golf Tour Company

With all these previous questions asked and answered, your party should at least consider engaging one of the numerous Ireland-based golf tour companies that can help you book a once-in-a-lifetime (or maybe a first-in-a-lifetime) tour in Ireland. If you engage one, we recommend that you choose a company that is actually based in Ireland or one with an affiliated office there. Some less reputable companies will book a tour for a group over the Internet and then just mark it up. Of course, you can accomplish the same result without this "middle-man" fee. If you do choose to use a tour company, check its background and get credible references before sending the deposit.

Following is a list of Irish golf tour operators that are members of the Ireland Golf Tour Operators' Association (IGTOA), also known as *The Voice for Irish Golf Tourism*. This association represents most of the Irish-based tour operators who provide a broad range of golf tours and related activities. Members of IGTOA are the market leaders in the Irish golf tourism industry and they deliver on their promises. Visit **www.igtoa.com** for detailed information on the organization and reasons why you should choose an IGTOA member to help with your golf tour. There is also an interactive map on this site that shows the location of 62 golf courses throughout the island.

IGTOA Current Members

Adams & Butler	**www.irishluxury.com**
Carr Golf & Corporate Travel	**www.carrgolf.com**
Celtic Golf	**www.celticgolf.com**
Eire Golf	**www.irelandscotlandgolf.com**
Golf and Incentive Travel	**www.incentive-travel.com**
Golf Vacations Ireland	**www.golf-irl.com**
Ireland Golf	**www.irelandgolf.com**
Irish Pro Golf Tours	**www.irishprogolftours.com**
JD Golf Tours	**www.jdgolf.ie**
Specialty Ireland Tours Ltd	**www.specialityireland.com**
Traveling the Fairways	**www.ttfgolf.com**

Tailor-Made Golf Tours	**www.tailormadegolftours.com**
Easi Golf	**email: easigolf@gofree.indigo.ie**
Galway Bay Golf Holidays	**www.irishgolf.de**
Golf & Events	**email: gei@eircom.net**

Other Ireland Based Tour Companies

Great Northern Ireland	**www.greatnortherntravelandtours.co.uk**
Irish Golf Tours Ltd	**www.irishgolftours.com**
Ovation Group	**www.ovation.ie**
Southwest Ireland Golf, Ltd (SWING)	**www.swinggolfireland.com**

Tour Companies prominent in the American Market

The Old Course Experience	**www.oldcourse-experience.com**
Perry Travel	**www.perrygolf.com**

III.

ABOUT IRELAND—What You Should Know

"A Boxty in the Oven,
A Boxty in the Pan,
If You Can't Make a Boxty,
You'll Never Get a Man"
Author unknown

HERE IS SOME background information on Ireland and what you can expect when you travel there. We have included dozens of pertinent websites in the Appendix at the back of the book in addition to the ones provided here. They are some of the best sources for detailed and up-to-date news and travel information. Be sure to check the Irish newspaper websites (also in the Appendix) as you get closer to your departure date for the most current information on the areas you will be visiting to play golf or sightsee. As we have said before, thorough planning is the key to a successful tour.

An important part of your preparation is to study the geography of the destination and to be aware and knowledgeable of the political boundaries of those regions. To help you be a better guest in Ireland and have a more enjoyable trip, this chapter will help you learn some basic facts about the country.

The Island of Ireland

For starters, you need to know that Ireland is an island separated from the larger island of Great Britain; for travelers, the two are physically connected only by ferries and airlines. The island is composed of The Republic of Ireland (the capital is Dublin), and Northern Ireland (the capital is Belfast). Both are English speaking European countries.

The United Kingdom and Northern Ireland

The *United Kingdom* consists of England, Wales, Scotland and Northern Ireland. *Great Britain* is the large island that contains England, Wales, and Scotland, while Northern Ireland is on the island of Ireland. These countries *have not* adopted the Euro as its currency and the British Pound Sterling (£) is the currency in use. Be aware that the banks in Northern Ireland *also print their own version of the UK currency.*

The Republic of Ireland is politically separate from the United Kingdom in more ways than one. Importantly, the Republic belongs to the European Union (EU) and adopted the Euro (€) as its currency. Although the United Kingdom is a member of the EU, it decided to hold onto its own currency instead of adopting the Euro.

TIP: be careful to acknowledge these distinctions when talking with your Irish hosts so that you don't call them British or English or part of the UK. And don't refer to your hosts from Northern Ireland as British or English. After all, as a U.S. citizen, you would think it strange if a visitor wasn't sure if you were a citizen of Canada or Mexico!

Geography, Population and Demographics

The island of Ireland is divided into four historic provinces-Ulster, Munster, Leinster, and Connacht—and 32 counties, of which 26 are in the Republic of Ireland and six (all part of Ulster) are in Northern Ireland. The Republic of Ireland is a parliamentary democracy headed by the President of Ireland. Northern Ireland has its own regional/local government and is part of the United Kingdom.

The population of the island in 2010 was about 6.3 million with approximately 4.5 million living in the Republic of Ireland and about 1.8 million in Northern Ireland. Over half the people on the island are under 30 years old and there is a slight diversity of ethnic groups and cultures.

87.4% Irish
7.5% various Caucasian/white
1.3% Asian
1.1% African descent/black
1.1% mixed ethnicities
1.6% unspecified

Ireland has the fastest growing population in Europe with a high birth rate of 16.8 children per 1,000 inhabitants in 2010, compared with a EU average of 10.7 children per 1,000 inhabitants. Approximately 10% of Ireland's population is comprised of foreign citizens.

Area

The Republic of Ireland is 486 kilometers (304 miles) long and 275 kilometers (172 miles) wide, or 70,282 square kilometers (27,136 square miles). It is just a little larger than the state of West Virginia or maybe Rhode Island, Vermont, New Hampshire, and Massachusetts combined. Another way to look at it is that Ireland can actually fit into the state of Texas ten times over. The Republic of Ireland occupies 84% of the 84,421 sq. km island while Northern Ireland occupies the other 16%. Visit **www.gov.ie** for detailed information on the geography of Ireland.

The capital of the Republic of Ireland is the city of Dublin (from Dubh Linn meaning "black pool"). In a 2010 estimate, Dublin's population was recorded to be just over 500,000, but the greater metropolitan region's is about 1.2 million. People who live within 100 km or 62 miles of the center of Dublin comprise 25% of the Republic's entire population. For more information on Dublin, including its history, culture, government, and economy visit **www. en.wikipedia.org/wiki/dublin.**

The capital of Northern Ireland is Belfast (from the Irish Beal Feirste, meaning "mouth of the sandbars"). With a population of 267,000, Belfast is the largest city in Northern Ireland. With a population of about 500,000, the metropolitan area is the second largest on the island. Unfortunately, Belfast has a sad history as it saw the worst of the conflicts in Ireland in the 1970s, with nearly half of the total deaths in the time of the "Troubles" occurring inside the city. Thankfully, since the Good Friday Agreement of 1998, there has been significant urban regeneration in the city centre.

For more information on Belfast, visit **www. en.wikipedia.org/wiki/belfast**.

History

The history of Ireland is fascinating and it's a good idea to read up on it, just as you would for any country you plan to visit. We recommend **www.en.wikipedia.org/wiki/ republic_of_ireland** as a good source for a concise history of the Republic of Ireland. Wikipedia will also provide you with as much statistical information as you can use, and other relevant information about the country.

Religion

About 87% of the population of the Republic of Ireland is Roman Catholic and various Protestant groups (Church of Ireland, Presbyterian, and Methodist) total 4%. In Northern Ireland, 53% are Protestant and 44% are Catholic. Islam is the third largest group in the Republic but constitutes only 0.7% of the population.

Land Use

Agriculture is the primary category of land use in Ireland. About 10% of the land area is comprised of forests, most of which are intended for commercial use and consist of homogenous species. The only place you can see a native forest area is in one of the national parks in Ireland. Otherwise, rural land is being converted through the rapid urbanization that is occurring in the Dublin area.

Climate

> *"There is no such thing as bad weather, just bad clothing"*
>
> *Geir Vic*

Ireland has a mild temperate climate with an average summer temperature of 57°F/12°C. Average temperatures in spring and fall are 50°F/10°C and in winter 43°F/6°C. Snow is rare but rain showers can occur at any time of the year.

Although the weather is subject to frequent changes, there are few occurrences involving extreme temperatures. Depending on where you live in the U.S., you may initially find the weather in Ireland a bit uncomfortable, but you will soon adapt. To put it simply, be prepared for changeable weather and proper planning and provision is a must.

Although rain is experienced year round, the wettest period is from August to January. There is normally only one 30-40 day period from mid-December to mid-January when plants don't bloom. Spring is a beautiful time to be in Ireland.

Search the web for "weather in Ireland" for all the information you'll need, or visit **www.weather.com** for current weather conditions and 10-day forecasts. You can also check out **www.expatfocus.com/ireland_weather** for a guide to weather and climate in Ireland.

For current weather information in Northern Ireland, go to the website maintained by the UK's National Weather Service, also called the "Met Office," at **www.metoffice. gov.uk** and **www.weather.ie** for forecasts about conditions in Ireland.

IV.

THE HISTORY OF IRISH GOLF

"Maireann croi eadrom i bh fad"
A merry heart lives long.

Irish proverb

Stick and Ball Games—Did They Start in Ireland?

As both golf and the traditional Irish sport of hurling are stick and ball affairs, some have gone as far to suggest that the Royal and Ancient game may have been played on the Emerald Isle long before the Scots or Saxons took to it with such relish.

Researching the centenary history of the great County Meath links, Laytown and Bettystown a few years ago, Brian Keogh discovered a note in the club records that gave credence to this theory and even went as far to suggest mythological Irish heroes such as Fionn Mac Cumhaill and Cu Chulainn had bashed a few long drives in their day.

"Some might say that golf is a foreign game," the club secretary Stephen Henly told the Annual General Meeting in 1939. "But Mr. Delany would tell them that it was a good old Irish game and that it was played by Fionn MacCumhaill and Cu Chulainn long before St Andrews was ever heard of."

One suspects that Mr. Henly had his tongue firmly planted in his cheek, but it's a debate that has never gone away and it never fails to rile our Celtic cousins in Scotland.

On the 18th green at Laytown and Bettystown Golf Club, County Meath, in the club's inaugural season (1909). The photograph was taken from the tall dunes that protect the wonderful finishing hole.

Photo Credit: Laytown and Bettystown Golf Club

According to the Golfing Union of Ireland, **www.gui.ie,** it all started on a sand dune on the eastern coast of Scotland, in the Kingdom of Fife, during the 15th Century. When James VI of Scotland became James I of England in 1603, he brought to England with him a love of golf that he would share with his new Kingdom. With his royal endorsement, this recreational sport craze spread throughout the rest of Europe and eventually the whole world. James brought the sport to Ireland to a settlement just east of Belfast called

'Laird of Braidstone' near Ayr and the Prestwick golf links, inspiring play. He also settled the 'Plantation of Ulster' in 1609 that consisted mostly of Scotch Presbyterians, many of them avid golfers. This helped to sow the seeds of golf in Ireland.

"Ancient Irish Sports"

Around 1911, a fascinating piece on the origins on Irish golf appeared in *The Irish Times*' "Golfing Gossip" column. The correspondent, known to us only as "Traveller", recalled how a Ballybunion golfer gave up the game on being told "no good Irishman would be seen playing the games of the foreigner."

Imagine his delight when he came across a book at a stall on Dublin's Aston Quay, hard by the River Liffey, which was once a haven of second-hand bookshops. Its title was "Ancient Irish Sports" and to his amazement he found a whole chapter was devoted to golf, which the author had described as "one of the ancient games of the Gael."

Word on the book's contents spread like wildfire in Ballybunion and as a result, the banned game was included in the list of Irish games that all good Irishmen were permitted to play and he, and many others, were able to resume their places on the links.

The Irish Times correspondent was distraught when he lost his copy of the tome, which claimed (somewhat outlandishly) that Ireland's St Columbcille (521-597 AD)—the founder of the great monastery on the Isle of Iona in the Scottish Inner Hebrides—had played golf in his time.

"The last golfer who got hold of (the book) was an officer in the Munsters under orders for France," wrote

Traveller. "He brought it with him to finish reading it in his spare hours at the front. He was killed soon after his arrival "o'er there" and in all probability the book, with the precious secret it contained, lies buried and beyond all hope of recovery, in what was once the dug-out of a British soldier."

The "Black Watch" and Irish Golf

In 1762, Ireland's first golf club was established in Bray, just south of Dublin. In 1881, Royal Belfast was formed and is one of the oldest golf clubs in the world. There are 40 golf clubs in the United Kingdom, on the island of Ireland and around the world that have been granted Royal status by the British Monarchy. The Scottish military also had a huge influence on the establishment of many golf clubs in Ireland. These include The Island, The Curragh, Limerick, and Lahinch.

There is no doubt today that the establishment of golf in Ireland has its roots in the garrisons of British soldiers who played their part in the creation of clubs such as Lahinch on the Atlantic coast in County Clare. The great links, beloved of Phil Mickelson, date back to 1892 when an 18-hole course was laid out with the assistance of officers of the Limerick-based Scottish "Black Watch" regiment.

Trans-Atlantic Cable—Communication and Golf

The laying of the Trans-Atlantic Cable was another factor in the establishment of golf in Ireland. During the last half of the 19th century, two competing companies, Western Union and Commercial Cable Company, were laying the wires. These workers, who played golf in their homeland but couldn't find any courses in Ireland, started many of Ireland's golf courses. Telegraph workers who lived in a large company housing complex near Waterville built a nine hole golf course on the sand dunes in 1889 and thus laid the foundation for the Waterville Links Golf Club.

Golf—*A Way of Life* in Lahinch

Scotland has had its influence on establishing golf in Ireland. For example, Lahinch Golf Course set on the edge of the Atlantic Ocean is a jewel in a marvelous selection of Irish seaside courses. The Merchant Princes of Limerick assisted by officers of the famed Black Watch Regiment founded the Club on April 15, 1892.

Sir Alexander Shaw, a wealthy Limerick bacon curer, and some friends decided that the ground at Lahinch would make an excellent golf links and sent to St Andrews for the celebrated Scottish golf professional "Old" Tom Morris, who cut the tops off some of the sand hills to construct greens and tees and fill the hollows. Then the canny Scot stood back and declared: "You have the finest links it has ever been my good fortune to play over. It can be classed with the five best in the United Kingdom."

From its earliest days, Lahinch enjoyed a national and international reputation as being a wonderful test of seaside golf. For over 100 years, there has been a wonderful interaction between the Club and the village. Of course, Ireland would not remain part of the United Kingdom for much longer and golf soon shook off its reputation as a game for the British elite and became a hallowed past time for Irishmen from all walks of life.

Dr Alister MacKenzie, the Scottish course designer (and co-creator of Augusta National Golf Club) began a major reconstruction of Lahinch in 1927. By this time Ireland had achieved her independence from the United Kingdom, leading to the establishment of the Republic of Ireland in 1949.

Despite high levels of emigration and widespread poverty, golf grew in popularity all over the country and Lahinch became a perfect example of the game's newfound stature as a sport for all. Given the Scottish influence on the town, Lahinch has become known as the St Andrew's of Ireland. In the village, golf is not just a tradition, but also *a way of life*. Everybody plays the game, or talks about golf or the weather.

John Burke was the greatest golfer ever to come out of Lahinch. Burke was a Walker Cup representative in 1933 and won 26 amateur championships, nine of them at the national level. He was also a character in the mold of Mick O'Loughlin, a butcher from Ennistymon. The pair met in a now famous rivalry in the South of Ireland championship, hosted by Lahinch since 1895. Once, when the butcher looked like he was beating his opponent, Burke, knowing Mick's weakness, dropped a half-a-crown into a bunker where the other ball had gone. Mick saw the coin shining in the sunlight, put it in his pocket and then, played a perfect shot to the pin and got the putt. As O'Laughlin had his hand out for the wager, Burke replied, "I won the hole! You removed something from the hazard before playing the ball."

The Golfing Union of Ireland

The oldest such organization in the world, The Golfing Union of Ireland was formed October 12th of 1891. The nine original clubs that made up this Union were all located in the northern province of Ulster. Not long after, in 1893, the Ladies Golf Union was formed along with the Irish Ladies Golf Union.

The 1960 World Cup at Portmarnock Golf Club attracted golfers from around the world and was a major factor in erupting the golf scene throughout Ireland. Golf courses and clubs sprung up all over the island to accommodate the growing demand. Presently there are around 400 affiliated clubs in Ireland, catering to well over 200,000 golfers. The Golfing Union of Ireland even began providing financial assistance for building pay-as-you-go courses around Ireland.

To maintain a high standard of golf in Ireland, the Golfing Union, through their Coaching Management Committee, offers regular training and coaching sessions for both the young and the old. Interclub tournaments are also organized on a regular basis to ensure a high level of competition for any handicap.

Men and women from all walks of life love Irish golf. And there are roughs aplenty waiting to show you some Irish hospitality.

Note: Rev. Fr. Enda Glynn, the official historian of Lahinch Golf Club, contributed to this section.

V.

PLAY GOLF THE IRISH WAY with Brian Keogh

"To play the game is great; to win the game is greater; to love the game is the greatest"
Author unknown

FINALLY, YOU'RE IN Ireland, you're rested, you're confident about your golf and knowledge of the country and you know you will have a great Irish Experience. You're on the first tee box and . . . *It's Time to Tee Off!*

Statue of Payne Stewart at Waterville Golf Club
Photo Credit: Waterville Golf Club

When I (Bill Ruskin) decided to write *The American Golfer's Guide to Ireland*, I knew how to provide information that could help golfers plan successful and memorable tours to the island of Ireland. But I couldn't advise them on how to play golf once they arrived there. I needed to connect with a native, a lifelong Irish golfer, who could advise Yankee golfers how to play some of the best courses in the world, and for a short time in their lives become Irish while doing it. After a lengthy search, Seamus Smith, General Secretary of the Irish Golfing Union, informally introduced me via the Internet to Brian Keogh, a well-known freelance golf writer residing in Dublin. I contacted him in the middle of the 2010 professional golf circuit and he agreed to contribute the following excellent section of this guide. At the time, I didn't realize the other huge commitments Brian had made, including his obligations to his family with a new baby, the pressure of travel and following professional tournaments around the world. For the next seven months or so as Brian and I communicated about his text, I would get an *iPhone* response from the USA, Spain, Scotland or wherever he was writing about a golf event. Impatiently, I contacted Brian several times concerned about the delay in getting his text and his replies were always prompt and reassuring, "the text is well underway" or "keep the faith." I did, and as you are about to read, it was well worth the wait. This important segment of the book and Brian's writing skills will vicariously transport you to Ireland and the golf courses you have been dreaming about playing there.

Play Golf the Irish Way *With Brian Keogh*

Strangers Are Friends That Haven't Met

There are stuffy golf clubs all over the world, places of privilege where the ordinary Joe will never tread unless he's fitting new tiles in the showers or dropping someone there in his taxi.

Thankfully for lovers of the Irish game, those places are rare on the Emerald Isle, where strangers are simply friends that haven't met yet.

Ireland is not known as the land of a hundred thousand welcomes for nothing and wherever you choose to play, you're guaranteed to make friends and many of them.

Take Lahinch, known far and wide as the St Andrews of Ireland, given the role that men such as the legendary "Old" Tom Morris or Augusta National designer Alister MacKenzie played in creating the wonderful County Clare links, just a few miles from the world famous Cliffs of Moher.

Many visitors had the pleasure of playing golf there with the legendary Ennistymon butcher Mick O'Loughlin, who was a fine amateur golfer in his day. Years ago, when a couple of American visitors asked about the chance of a game with some of the local members, club secretary Brud Slattery offered to join them, adding: "And I'll send one of the caddies up to the village to fetch the butcher." O'Loughlin duly arrived, wiping his hands on his bloody apron before removing it for battle. After a few holes, one of the bemused visitors turned to Slattery and whispered: "Say, if the local butcher is so readily available to play golf, he sure can't make much money." To which 'Brud' replied: "No, but he sure makes a lot of friends."

That anecdote says it all about Ireland, which had more than 400 golf clubs at the end of 2010. That may not seem like a great number compared to the 18,000 or so to be found in the United States. After all, Ireland is smaller in area than Indiana and only slightly larger than South Carolina. It would be naive to think you're going to see it all on a short trip. It is a pretty small place until you get into a hire car. Yet that's where the real fun starts according to multiple major champion Pádraig Harrington, who knows every back road and boreen (a little road or laneway) of Ireland as well as he knows the manicured fairways of Augusta National.

Padraig Harrington's Advice on Playing Golf in Ireland

He's Ireland's official golfing ambassador and many of the people who join him for pre-tournament pro-ams around the world are planning to visit Ireland for that golfing trip of a lifetime.

So what kind of advice does he give them?

"It all depends," says Pádraig, who's traveled all over the 32 counties, 26 in the Republic of Ireland and six north of the border, since his amateur days.

"This is a once in a lifetime trip for most people and many of them have been saving up for years."

As a qualified accountant, Harrington knows that finance plays a crucial role in planning any major venture.

"A lot of what you might plan to do is determined by your budget. But the most important thing to remember is that road maps can be deceptive! If you can, hire a driver to take you from golf course to golf course. If you can't, remember that if the course you want to play is 60 miles away on a map, that doesn't necessarily mean you are going to get there in 45 minutes.

"But that's the beauty of Ireland. You could head north from Dublin [Republic of Ireland] for a game at Royal County Down [Northern Ireland] and end up stopping off at Baltray, which is about halfway up the coast outside Drogheda. Not many people know that you can get a room in the clubhouse and stay the night there. And the Boyne salmon in the restaurant is famous.

"Planning what to do when you finally make that trip all depends on your expectations. The scenery in the Northwest of Ireland, say Donegal and Sligo, is what many people imagine Ireland to be like. My advice is to stick with the B&B's in that part of the country because you are going to get great value."

Rule 27—*The Ban*

American visitors may be astounded to learn that until as recently as 1971, members of the Gaelic Athletic Association (GAA)—the governing body for the traditional Irish sports of Gaelic Football and Hurling—were banned from playing "foreign games" under threat of expulsion from the organisation.

Rule 27, or "The Ban," as it was infamously known, stated "any member of the association who plays or encourages in any way rugby, football, hockey or any imported game which is calculated to injuriously affect our national pastimes, is suspended from the association."

It didn't stop sports lovers from risking their GAA futures and many surreptitiously continued to play the "foreign" games under assumed names. Take the case of Peter Gordon Kerins, who came from a Kerry family steeped in the traditions of the GAA. Seven of his brothers won Kerry County championship medals and he was tipped for Kerry football stardom early in his career before he received a letter from his GAA club in 1966, stating that he must "write a letter apologising for playing soccer with Tralee Dynamos."

He never wrote the letter and went on to become a legend of Kerry soccer. But he would have had fewer problems had he limited his non-GAA sporting activities to golf, which became accepted as legitimate sport for a proud Irishman given its Celtic origins, across the water in Scotland.

Ireland and the USA—Golfing Enclaves, Poles Apart

The Dublin playwright George Bernard Shaw claimed, "England and America are two countries divided by a common language." He could just as easily have swapped England for his native Ireland and had he been writing about the golfing experience in both lands, he would have been spot on, too.

Despite the proliferation of American-style golfing enclaves that have mushroomed all over the country in recent years, not to mention the vast improvements in levels of service, things are still far more rough and ready in Ireland than they are in the United States.

The biggest difference golfers will discover is the weather, which is predictably unpredictable. It rains between 150 and 225 days a year so don't forget your waterproofs. Atlantic frontal systems travel northeast over the island, which means you are more likely to get drowned on the west coast than the east.

The good news is that the rain makes Ireland a green and pleasant land and you are unlikely to meet too many fair-weather golfing types.

Golf Courses Abound—Visit Ireland and Play

Ireland had 430 golf courses at the end of 2010, a huge increase on the 275 you could play in 1990. The boom has been great for golfers but bad for business as there are simply too many courses and too few golfers.

For example, 100 courses are within an hour's drive of The K Club, the Arnold Palmer designed course that hosted the 2006 Ryder Cup. As a result, membership dues and greens fees have fallen, which is great news for tourists.

Most overseas visitors come to Ireland to play our links courses. There are approximately 150 true links courses in the world and Ireland can claim nearly a third of the total with Royal County Down, Royal Portrush and The European Club regarded as some of the best golf courses anywhere.

Ireland has 50 true links courses, which means there are another 380 parkland courses to be explored, many of them world class. Wherever you choose to play, you will find that the best days of the week to tee it up are Wednesday, Thursday and Friday. The members pack the courses at weekends, Monday is a popular day for golf society outings and Tuesday is traditionally "ladies day" at many clubs.

If you are traveling to Ireland during the summer months (warning, the term 'summer' may be misleading), many clubs organise an "Open Week." It does exactly what it says on the tin—competitions are open to anyone with an official handicap certificate from their golf federation and entry fees are usually modest.

The calendar of open weeks is available on the Golf Union of Ireland website **www.gui.ie/open_fixtures.asp**. It's a great way to see Irish golf clubs at their very best and you are sure to receive a very warm welcome from members who will be keen to hear what you think of their course.

Tips on Playing, Caddies, Golf Club Membership, Conduct

If you are visiting a golf club for the day and intend to have dinner or a bite to eat after your round, it's best to change in the locker room rather than your car unless you really are in a hurry to get away.

Do not wear, caps, hats or rain gear inside the clubhouse. Remove them before you leave the locker room.

Most clubs will provide fresh towels free of charge or for a modest fee and information is usually available from the caddie master or behind the bar in the case of smaller clubs.

Smart casual dress is required in all clubhouses while some clubs may insist that visitors wear a jacket and tie or a jacket and polo necked shirt in the bar or dining room, especially in the evenings.

Unless you are a doctor on call, do not use your mobile phone in the clubhouse. Due to the proliferation of these devices, many clubs have now set aside an area where members and guests can make or receive calls without disturbing others. If you must take your phone with you, make sure it is on vibrate. This way you can make your way to a designated area to take, or make, your call discreetly.

Play Golf Like the Irish

"Never play too much golf . . . two rounds a day is plenty"—Author unknown

General Guidelines

If you want to play golf like the Irish, there are a few rules to bear in mind. Insanity is a much loved trait, so don't be surprised if your Irish friends invite you out for a game in conditions that might make for breaking news on The Weather Channel back home. If Irish golfers worried about the weather, they would get about two games a year, so be prepared to man-up and get out there in a rainstorm and 40 mph winds.

Slagging, or pulling one's leg as it is more commonly known, is part and parcel of the Irish golf scene. If you have never been to Ireland before, be prepared to take plenty of good-humoured abuse, at all times.

Most club golfers in Ireland do not play stroke play golf with the general exception of the club championship. Stableford points are the usual form of combat and match play is a favourite. If you are playing a famous Irish links course, you may want to keep a card so that you can tell people that you broke 100, 90, etc. on a world famous track such as Royal County Down, Lahinch or Portmarnock. Unless you are a very good, single-digit handicapper, it is not recommended that you do this in a four ball [foursome] with Irish golfers as patience will wear thin as they watch you stalk the line of a two-footer for another quadruple bogey.

The Swing

Show me an Irish golfer with a textbook swing and I will show you a very rare bird indeed. Think of all the great Irish professional golfers and you will see that very few of them swing the club like Tiger Woods or Adam Scott. Rory McIlroy is the exception that proves the rule and if you look at the great Jimmy Bruen (famous for his "loop"), Padraig Harrington, Graeme McDowell or Eamonn Darcy, the hero of Europe's Ryder Cup victory at Muirfield Village in 1987, you will see that the Irish golfer has a very individual action. Darcy was once described as having a swing like a man "picking a five pound note from a grate with a tongs", but he was effective.

On seeing Darcy's unique swing at that Ryder Cup, one American remarked: "Eamonn shouldn't take that swing out of town too often—he might have trouble getting spare parts."

Some say that these odd swings are a result of taking up the game without any formal coaching, but a lot has to do with the weather. When you learn to play golf in wet and windy conditions, a tight, economic swing is absolutely crucial and a low-ball flight is guaranteed.

The English coach Simon Holmes, who has worked with some of the great of the game including Seve Ballesteros, has his own take on the subject.

"Eamonn Darcy and Padraig Harrington could hardly be described as orthodox, but they became fine ball-strikers," Holmes told The Irish Times' Dermot Gilleece in 1997. "In flat, calm conditions in Florida, the ball flight is considered to be very important. But in a 30 mph Irish wind, if you hit high shots with a beautiful-looking golf swing, you are not going to find the ball."

The Essence of Links Golf

If you're coming to Ireland to play golf, the chances are that you're really coming to play links golf. But what is links golf?

Padraig Harrington won back-to-back British Open titles in 2007 and 2008, so he knows what he's talking about:

"I would define links golf with a little story," Harrington said. "It was the Open at Royal Lytham in 2001. So on the 16th hole and I'm not doing so well, so I stand up, I take driver out, it's a blind tee shot and I ripped this drive over the hill, everything goes great, over the marker. There's not a sound from the spectators that are there, so over the hill I go. I start looking for my golf ball 120 yards short of the green in the right-hand trap of the fairway. I also looked in the left-hand trap. So I covered 120 yards to the pin and 60 yards wide. I must have covered an acre of ground and in the end; my ball is 15 feet from the hole in a bunker. That's links golf (laughter). That is exactly what links golf is. You hit it and it's still a mystery until you actually find your golf ball."

Largely treeless and exposed to the elements, a links golf course can change utterly from morning to afternoon. A hole that required a good drive, a three wood and a seven-iron to reach the green in the morning hole could require no more than a fairway wood and a nine iron to find the green if the wind changes direction in the afternoon.

"Links golf is meant to throw a few curve balls at you, to knock you off balance when you're out there," Harrington explained. "It's really more of a mental test than anything else."

No American has made the adjustment from American to links golf conditions as well as Tom Watson, who won the British Open five times and finished second to Stewart Cink after a play-off for the 2009 Open at Turnberry.

The man from Kansas City admits that it took him quite some time to adjust to the vagaries of the links game and while he had won the Open in 1975 and 1977, it was not until he played Ballybunion in County Kerry in 1981 that he really learned what it was all about.

"I think that kind of solidified my appreciation and love for the game," Watson said of his first visit to Ballybunion. "My understanding of links golf started in '79 and culminated in '81. Before '79, I didn't particularly like links golf. I was an American golfer. I liked it through the air, hit the ball high, couldn't hit the ball low with much accuracy.

"But I didn't like it. And I remember in '79 I said this many times that I played it; I played at Royal Lytham and St. Annes. I didn't play well in the tournament, but I had somewhat of a bad attitude. I got some bad bounces and this and that. And I finally told myself, you know, this game is played on the ground. And you have to expect some bounces, some good bounces and bad bounces. And I've had some terrible bounces out here. But I've had some great bounces.

"In '81 my friend Sandy Tatum organized a trip that took us first to Ballybunion, and that started my love affair with Ballybunion and links golf, side by side."

How to Tackle a Links

> *"If you are going to throw a club, it is important to throw it ahead of you, so you don't waste energy going back to pick it up."*
>
> *Tommy Bolt*

Golf is golf, no matter where you play. Right? Wrong. Playing golf in Ireland is a unique experience and Irish links courses will require you to play shots you've never played before.

It's not just the challenging weather conditions that make it so different but the very nature of the links game. The good news is that you are highly unlikely to find yourself blocked out by a tree, because there are very few on the exposed terrain. But you will have to learn to deal with things like gorse, ferns, marram grass, riveted bunkers, rabbit scrapes, sheep droppings, rabbit droppings, railway sleepers, heather and, above all, wind.

Here's a quick guide to some of the things you are likely to face and how to deal with them.

Bunkers

Links courses are littered with deep bunkers. Some of them are huge, imposing hazards that you can see from hundreds of yards away. Others are small, deviously disguised holes in the ground that you didn't even know existed until you discover your well-struck drive nuzzling the face of one of these beauties. Many are very deep indeed (several at the European Club have wooden steps to help you escape) and getting out first time can often present a major challenge, even if there are steps.

The sand in links bunkers is often very fine indeed, which means you are likely to find yourself plugged if the ball comes in from a great height. The golden rule with links bunkers is the same as it is for bunkers everywhere—make sure you escape first time.

If you are unlucky enough to find your ball up very close to the sheer face of a links bunker, trying to go forwards is tantamount to suicide. If possible, play out sideways or backwards and then take it from there. If you can't, take a penalty drop. You might make a bogey, or even a double bogey, but you are unlikely to rack up a huge number that will completely wreck your scorecard.

Turf

Firm, springy turf is one of the great joys of links golf and most courses consist of fine fescue surfaces that literally ring in summer when the terrain is firm and ball runs for a country mile. Unlike parkland fairways, the ball does not sit up like a coconut and you will find it a little intimidating at first, as you are forced to hit down on the ball to get a crisp strike.

Chipping and pitching off such tight surfaces can lead to a great deal of wear and tear on one's nerves but there is nothing as satisfying as nipping the ball cleanly off links turf.

With so many run offs around the greens at links courses, you will be faced with many challenging recovery shots. But the beauty of links turf is that barring the presence of an obstacle such as a bunker; you can use a straight-faced club or a putter to get the ball close from almost anywhere.

The *run up shot,* or *chip and run*, is a must-have shot on links courses and one worth practicing before you travel. Not only is it often the correct shot around the greens, it is also vital on windy days.

A high ball might be ideal in warm, virtually windless conditions. But when the wind is howling into your face, you must take spin off the ball to keep it under control and the low, punched approach often yields the best results.

Learning to 'chip' the ball from 120 yards with a six iron is a matter of feel and practice.

Greens

Links greens are generally a lot slower than the putting surfaces you will tackle at most high-end US courses. It's possible to make Irish links greens as fast as those at Augusta National but they would become unplayable in high winds. Contours vary from buried elephant to flat as a pancake but one thing is certain, the wind can become a factor.

Good links greens are a pleasure to putt until you are standing over a three footer in a 30 mph wind. You will be buffeted around, making a wider stance a must on such occasions. The ball is highly likely to move on very windy days, which makes learning to putt without grounding your putter a skill you may be forced to master to avoid a penalty.

The Wind Factor

Reading greens accurately is something that even the best players in the world find challenging. Flat links greens are even more perplexing but when you add in the wind factor, reading putts becomes even more important. Just ask Tom Watson.

"There's not too many trees on those links golf courses," Watson said. "None to be exact. You're fully exposed to the wind on a lot of the greens, and you definitely have to play the wind. You have to play the gusts sometimes. It feels like a three-inch break. No, now it's a six-inch break, now it's a two-inch break. This is all in the matter of a second before you play it."

Distance Control

Clubbing yourself correctly in a strong wind is another art form but as a general rule, you can add or subtract 10 yards for every 10 mph of wind speed. The air at sea level is highly resistant, which means that you may have to do some testing on the range to see exactly how far you hit the ball. Golfers who normally play in warm conditions in the US will find that they cannot hit the ball, as far in the cool, "thick" air you normally have to deal with at sea level. If you hit a seven iron 160 yards under normal conditions, you may find that your "Sunday best" is only traveling 145 yards in Irish conditions. Playing into a headwind, it will cost you even more yardage and it is not unusual to be forced to reach for a long-iron on a short par three when playing into the wind.

It's the opposite, of course, when the wind is behind you. However, controlling a ball downwind is infinitely more difficult and while you may be delighted to have no more than a nine-iron to the green for your second shot on a par-five, getting it to stop is another question entirely.

The temperature also affects the distance a ball will travel on a links course and Padraig Harrington used this knowledge to his advantage when he beat Sergio Garcia in a play-off for the 2007 (British) Open championship at Carnoustie. Having played in the Irish Professional Championship at The European Club the week before, Harrington knew exactly what to expect in terms of his distance control at the Scottish links.

"There's no question playing last week gave me an advantage," he said after picking up his first Claret Jug. "I got a couple of timely reminders at The European Club, just getting used to the fact that you could hit 7-iron into the wind and it's only going to go 125 yards. That just doesn't happen in our regular golf. We're used to hitting a 7-iron 180 yards into a slight breeze because it's warm. All of a sudden you go to a links course and that same little breeze is taking 20, 30 yards off the shot."

Harrington used that knowledge to his advantage at the first hole of a four-hole aggregate play-off, where he hit a seven iron to 15 feet and made birdie as Garcia came up short in a bunker and dropped a shot to fall a crucial two strokes behind straight away.

"I had 162 yards to the pin on the first playoff hole. I've got 7-iron in my hand because I know that while I'll normally hit it 180-yards, I'll be doing well to hit it 160 yards in cool conditions on a links course."

Shot-Making

There are dozens of shots worth perfecting before you tackle a links course but learning to keep the ball down when playing into the wind is a must. A high ball will balloon into the air and lose considerable distance, so tee the ball lower than normal when playing into the wind and swing easier. You are not going to hit the ball as far as you normally do, but an easy swing will impart less spin and allow the ball to bore through the wind.

The *punch shot* and the *low runner* are stock shots that you will use time and again. To play the low running shot, position the ball back in your stance, choke down on the club and make an abbreviated backswing. By holding the clubface low through impact, you will generate over spin and send the ball rolling hard towards the green. Naturally, this requires a great deal of practice to execute consistently but you will thoroughly enjoy trying to perfect it and the odd shot that comes off perfectly will make it all worthwhile.

"If it's windy and you want to drive, drop a couple and use a five."

A group of junior golfers on the first tee at Laytown and Bettystown Golf Club in 1949. This club in County Meath became a popular holiday destination for Irish families in the years after the Second World War.

Photo Credit: Laytown and Bettystown Golf Club

Caddies

The caddie is a dying breed and while you will find experienced loopers to carry your bag (or even two bags) at courses such as Portmarnock, Royal County Down, Lahinch, Ballybunion or Doonbeg, they are the exception rather than the rule.

But if you are very lucky, you might just come across a future major champion making some extra pocket money to support his golfing career. During the Hyundai Tournament of Champions in Hawaii at the start of the 2011 PGA Tour season, two American fans approached US Open champion Graeme McDowell with a photograph.

"You caddied for us at Portrush in 1999," they said, brandishing a picture that showed a young McDowell standing between them.

"Though I caddied for quite a few Americans, meeting these guys again like this is a first for me," McDowell said. "I would have got about £50 plus a tip for carrying those two bags, which probably represented my pocket-money back then for playing in an event like the Leinster Youths. An occasional caddying job in between practice. Now I'm playing here for more than a million dollars."

Caddies don't expect to earn a fortune from their duties but rates at the top courses will vary, depending on the seniority of the bagman. Anyone who has ever played a tough links course with the help of a local caddie will tell you that it's worth every cent. The lack of definition on a links course can make it tough to pick lines but a good caddie will save you plenty of strokes and you are unlikely to lose many balls.

Don't Blame Your Caddie

Of course, *blaming your caddie* for your own poor play is unlikely to do you much good. A struggling golfer was becoming increasingly frustrated by the pathetic standard of his play and eventually decided that there was nothing left other than to blame his frequent mistakes on his hapless caddie.

As the round ended, he turned to his man and said: "You have to be the worst caddie in the entire world." The caddie's reply has entered golfing lore, for he answered: "I don't think so, sir. That would be too much of a co-incidence."

One Too Many Aces

Of course, caddies will do just about anything to secure a handsome reward for their labours and it came to light many years ago that the caddies at Lahinch had gone a little too far. The par-three fifth at the County Clare links, known as The Dell, is completely blind with players forced to aim at a white stone on the top of the massive dune that squats in front of the green. Caddies would often volunteer to go ahead to the green, just in case their employer's ball should stray off-line in the rough. Caddying for a well-heeled American promised rich rewards should he make a hole in one and so it became common practice for caddies to put any ball that came even remotely near the flag into the hole before jumping up and down, crying: "It's in, it's in." The club cottoned on to the practice when they realised that one too many aces had been recorded on the most famous par three at Lahinch.

Another Lahinch caddie recounts the story of the terrible golfer that subjected him to a tortuous round. At one point the ball lay about 180 yards from the green and as the golfer sized up his situation, he asked his caddie, "Do you think I can get there with a 5-iron?" The caddie replied, "Eventually."

In fairness, the caddies at Lahinch are a very respectable bunch and excellent at their jobs. Back in the early 1990s, a US visitor was so delighted with his round there that on walking off the 18th green, he paid his caddie $100, considerably more than the then customary charge of £12 (before the advent of the euro). The Irish Times reported:

"Then, as a totally unexpected bonus, the caddie was also given a present of the player's clubs, bag, shoes, wet-suit and indeed every piece of golfing apparel he had in his possession. Greater love hath no golfer than he . . . ."

VI.

SELECTED GOLF COURSES IN IRELAND

"Man blames fate for other accidents, but feels personally responsible when he makes a hole in one"
Martha Beckman

IRELAND HAS SOME of the best golf courses in the world, including this handful that every golfer should play before he goes to the 19th hole in the sky.

Playing the Greats

Royal County Down: Newcastle, County Down, Northern Ireland

Jack Nicklaus couldn't conquer it and neither could Tom Watson. The majestic, savage beauty of *Royal County Down* should have been enough of a hint. This is a thinking man's links but even the shrewdest players ever to play the game were flummoxed by the guile of what is arguably *Irish golf's finest course*. The American Walker Cup team, featuring future PGA Tour stars Dustin Johnson and Rickie Fowler, claimed victory there in 2007. And they did it on a course that was designed before the advent of the bulldozer.

Modern equipment has made many great courses virtually obsolete in recent years but the links at Newcastle defies graphite, the ProV1 and anything else that modern golf cares to throw at it. Rather than trying to overpower the course, golf's future superstars were forced to play it with the sensitivity of a virtuoso violinist because it is a unique test in the game with its myriad blind shots, subtle run-offs and fringe-topped bunkers.

Whether the wind whips in from Dundrum Bay, screams up the coast from Baltray or wafts over the mountains of Mourne and down to the sea, it provides a stern test indeed.

Nicklaus found the gorse and bunker protected, par-five 18th particularly difficult to play, pointing out that anything hit left off the tee or with the second shot was tantamount to golfing suicide.

"You may as well go to the clubhouse or the airline booth and get a ticket home because you just can't hit it there," Nicklaus said during the 2001 Senior British Open, where he tied for sixth. "Unless I drive the ball far enough to where I could play an iron into that green, which means the wind would have to come behind me a bit, I would hit iron off the tee."

England's Gary Wolstenholme, who won five Walker Cup caps and two British Amateur Championships before turning professional at the age of 50, described the course as something akin to an Irish version of St Andrews or Royal St Georges.

"Sometimes you get some funny bounces and you have just got to accept it," he said. "If you make a mistake, you are working very hard to retrieve par or make a bogey. It is just like Augusta in some respects. Bobby Jones designed Augusta with St Andrews in mind and is quite unique. If you are not in the right place, getting yourself out of trouble is really hard. Because the greens are slightly raised, it makes it very difficult. Even if you miss a green pin high, it is actually harder than if you are at the front of a green."

Wolstenholme must have been listening to Ulsterman Ronan Rafferty, whose Walker Cup appearance came alongside current captain Colin Dalgleish at Cypress Point in 1981. The Warrenpoint man was the youngest ever Walker Cup player at the time and he was called in specially by the skipper Colin Dalgleish to give Great Britain and Ireland's Walker Cup young guns his expertise on how to play the course.

"I found myself telling the guys to hit it safe to the middle of the green here, safe to the middle of the green there," Rafferty said. "And you can see that the kids today play a different style of game. They play aggressive and you can't be aggressive round here. So it is a matter of taking somebody from that kind of game and bringing him or her back and showing them you can get the ball close to the hole with a little punched seven iron from 120 yards rather than a nine-iron or a wedge.

"That is why I say it's a negative golf course. There is lots of pull back and play safe. I found myself saying things like "never hit it past the centre of the green." There are runways in from 20 yards and 30 yards short of most greens here. Now if you are standing 140 yards away from a pin that is dangling the carrot right there in front of you and you have a nine-iron, it is very difficult to say, let's chip it 100 yards and run it up there.

"With no disrespect at all to the players, they are all very talented, it is not their style. This is not their style of golf course and they have got to adapt to it. This golf course doesn't compromise; they have to.

"The last few holes are killers. The 15th. Then 16, you are standing 50 yards short of the green thinking, this is a hard shot. The 17th suddenly becomes hard and 18, well, I remember during the seniors here, they were hitting irons off the tee and still had no idea how to get it up there."

Voted the world's best course outside the United States by Golf Digest magazine, it almost defies description in terms of its beauty. But the late Peter Dobereiner, one of golf's finest chroniclers, managed to do it justice. "The essence of golf is to say that it enhances the feeling that it is good to be alive," he wrote. "That's the first priority and absolute justification. The links of Royal County Down are exhilarating even without a club in your hand. This strip of dune land was 90 percent along on the road to being a golf course long before the game was invented."

Portmarnock: County Dublin

When you tee it up at *Portmarnock*, not only are you set to play at the most exclusive private golf club in the Republic of Ireland, you are also about to follow in the footsteps of legends.

The great Arnold Palmer got his first taste of links golf at the Dublin club, situated on a two-mile long peninsula in Dublin bay, when he joined forces with Sam Snead to win the Canada Cup (now the World Cup) at the course in 1960.

The man who would go on to become the "King", arrived in Ireland for his first tournament appearance in Europe as the reigning Masters champion.

"It's the first time I've played a course like this one," he said. "I've learned a lot of shots. Shots I've never played before in my life."

Palmer, who would go on to play in his first Open Championship at St Andrews the following week, finished tied for third in the individual tournament as the USA took the title with eight strokes to spare.

The renowned Irish golf writer Dermot Gilleece recalled Ireland's first staging of the 1960 Canada Cup as a turning point for golf in Ireland in a piece published in The Irish Times in 1999.

He wrote: "If the celebrated North Dublin links was new to many of the competing players, it had long been a favourite of Bernard Darwin's, the father-figure of golf writers. From first sight, he had been captivated by its location within the curve of coastline, where Howth Hill rises against the eastern skies and Ireland's Eye and Lambay Island stand sharp from the deep seas. There, the links evolved on a narrow tongue of shallow duneland running parallel to the mainland, with water on three sides."

Writing in the commemorative programme, Darwin said: "I think it is now 54 years since I first saw Portmarnock. It was in many respects a different course from that of today, but it still possesses the same charming qualities, the lovely turf, the wildness and solitude, the obvious golfing mixture, the sandhills and the sea.

"In those days, one did not drive round by a good road to get there, one sailed there across a stretch of water and I remember making the voyage in a high wind and a snowstorm and being a poor sailor, rejoicing when I was safely over."

There are no hidden dangers waiting to shipwreck a good round at Portmarnock, for one of the beauties of the course is that it is all there in front of you. It has stood the test of time, hosting 75 championships at amateur and professional level since 1899, when the legendary Harry Vardon competed in Portmarnock's first staging of the Irish Amateur Open.

In 1927, Scotland's George Duncan famously covered his body in brown paper to protect himself from the elements in the final round of the Irish Open. His winning 74 was carded in atrocious weather conditions and was described as "the greatest round in the circumstances in the history of golf" by the runner up, Henry Cotton.

The links would go on to host many more Irish Opens with the list of winners that looks like a who's who of golf with Bobby Locke, Ben Crenshaw, Hubert Green, Seve Ballesteros, Bernhard Langer, Ian Woosnam, José María Olazábal, and Michael Campbell on the roll of honour.

Palmer called the short 15th the best par three in the world and Crenshaw would suffer there en route to his Irish Open victory in 1976.

With four holes to play, he led Billy Casper and Brian Barnes by three shots but visited the Valley of Sin left of the 15th green and made a double bogey five that reduced his commanding lead to a single stroke. Gentle Ben recovered brilliantly, finishing par, par, birdie for a two-stroke win. "The toughest par-five I ever played," he said of the 15th afterwards.

Portmarnock hosted the Walker Cup in 1991 when Phil Mickelson and David Duval helped the United States beat Great Britain and Ireland 14-10 much to the disappointment of the Irish members of the home team—Padraig Harrington, Paul McGinley and Garth McGimpsey.

A detailed guide to tackling the links would be out of place here but suffice to say that Tom Watson found it a serious challenge.

"There are no tricks or nasty surprises, only an honest, albeit searching test of shot making skills," Watson said after a visit to the course.

Unlike many traditional links courses, where the front and back nines run parallel to one another, the holes at Portmarnock constantly change direction.

The doyen of American golf writer's, Herbert Warren Wind, attended the 1960 Canada Cup and opened his report for *Sports Illustrated* with the following description:

> *"The eighth Canada Cup match, which the American team of Sam Snead and Arnold Palmer won by the comfortable margin of eight shots, was played at Portmarnock, in the dune lands near Dublin, and while there are those who hold that among Irish courses both Newcastle County Down and Portrush are superior, a great many more insist that Portmarnock is not only Ireland's finest course but one of the four best tests of golf in the British Isles—along with St Andrews (where Arnold Palmer competes in the British Open this week), Muirfield and Hoylake. The majority of Portmarnock's holes are tucked in the folds between the dunes or separated by sharp ridges of rough. What makes the course fearsome, aside from its length (7,093 yards), is the combination of heavy swirling winds and the formidable rough—a thick growth of seaside grass, creeping willow, ferns, yarrow and countless wild rosebushes."*

The course now measures 7,382 yards for those bold enough to play from the championship tees. Just watch out for the estuary on the right when you play the recently redesigned opening hole. And enjoy Crenshaw's "par-five" 15th.

Royal Portrush: **County Antrim, Northern Ireland**

If you are looking for an excuse to play the Dunluce links at *Royal Portrush*, consistently ranked amongst the best courses in the world, then whiskey could be the answer because they've been distilling 'Old Bushmills' just four miles down the road for the past 400 years.

A drop or two of the hard stuff might be just what you need to keep the cold away as you tackle the famous links where the flamboyant Max Faulkner won the only (British) Open staged outside mainland Britain in 1951.

"Portrush stands on a rocky promontory that juts out into the Atlantic," wrote Bernard Darwin in *The Golf Courses of the British Isles*, first published in 1910. "The scenery of the coast is wonderfully striking. On the east are the White Rocks, tall limestone cliffs that lead to Dunluce Castle and the headlands of the Giant's Causeway. On the west are the hills of Inishowen, beyond which lie Portsalon and Buncrana and the links of Donegal."

American golfers may already be familiar with Royal Portrush following the 2010 US Open at Pebble Beach, where Portrush native Graeme McDowell became the first European for 40 years to lift the title.

McDowell learned the game on Portrush's second course, the less challenging but still wonderfully enjoyable Valley Course and owns a penthouse apartment overlooking the Dunluce links, which is the jewel in the crown and the course that helped Ryder Cup star and 2011 Open champion Darren Clarke fall madly in love with the game.

"If I had my choice as to what kind of golf I'd play, I'd like to play links golf every day," Clarke said. "I just like hitting a 5-iron from 140 yards, if you have to. Putting from 20 yards off the green. Things like that."

A Harry Colt masterpiece, the Dunluce is a serious test of golf, especially when the wind blows. And the wind blows almost all the time, which makes the feature hole an absolute terror. The par-three 14th, aptly named "Calamity Corner", measures 210 yards from the championship tee, requiring a long carry over a deep ravine. Anything drifting right will end up scuttling down a steep precipice onto the Valley Course below.

Bernardine Ruddy, Pat Ruddy, Tiger Woods, David Duval, Mark O'Meara and Scott McCarron at The European Club, Ruddy's incredible new golf facility in County Wicklow.

Photo Credit: The European Club

The European Club: **County Wicklow**

They say that owners come to resemble their dogs but in the case of The European Club, the most recent great links built in Ireland, the course simply reflects the designer's great love of the game.

Pat Ruddy has spent a lifetime in the game as a player, a golf writer and the designer of great courses such as the Glashedy Links at Ballyliffin, Druids Glen, Druids Heath, Port Salon, St. Margaret's, Donegal (Murvagh) and Montreal Island Golf Club, to name but a few.

Like many avid golfers, he dreamed of owning his very own course one day and he achieved that dream at Brittas Bay in County Wicklow, where he has carved a modern classic out of towering dunes on the shores of the Irish Sea.

The European Club is a wonderful test of golf that has flummoxed the best in the game from Tiger Woods and Padraig Harrington to new stars such as Rory McIlroy. If the rough is up and the wind is blowing hard, it is one hell of a test, especially if you choose the wrong set of tees.

Before you go out to play, you may be handed a scorecard and another card, bearing the words: Our Philosophy. In it, the owner tells us—

> *"Our approach to golf is fundamentalist. Accordingly, you will not find fussy furniture on our links. You might take it to be Spartan while we think it is akin to the way the game was at the beginning and, as it should be now. Take your clubs, card and pencil and go out and do battle with the golfscape that requires no artificial adornment."*

Humour is part and parcel of the game at The European Club, which the Ruddy family hopes will eventually become one of the great courses of the world. As you take your card in hand you might be struck by the following words, printed in bold, capital letters: "STAY AWAKE—GET AROUND IN 4-HOURS—YOU ARE AN ATHLETE!"

It might take you at little longer if you end up in some of the deep bunkers, which are made all the more menacing by railway sleepers. The sleepers have come in for a great deal of criticism but not only do they make it easier to maintain the bunkers, they also add to the feeling of intimidation on a course where optical illusion plays a major role.

Tiger Woods shot a course record 67 the day he visited The European Club. But even the world's best player was deceived by the design.

Playing the par-four 12th, which measured close to 460 yards, Woods asked the owner: "Is this a par-five?" Told it was a par four, he smiled and said: "Wow. What great optical illusions."

Who better to explain the design of the course that Pat Ruddy himself: "Care has been taken to conceal portions of fairways behind hillocks, in valleys and behind reeds (to induce panic in those who are weak of heart); to throw off depth perception by the use of swales (hiding a club length or more on many shots to the green); to exaggerate length by the use of long corridors through tall dunes (*like looking through the wrong end of a telescope . . . making relatively short shots into challenges of seeming gigantic proportions*); and to make some greens look extremely small by the simple device of making them wider, thus distorting the visual proportions, or placing them in front of high banks to give a misread of what the photographer would know as the "depth of field."

"The seventh hole, a par-4 of 470-yards, illustrates the design concept best. A small river hugs the fairway, and the green, all the way on the right. One doesn't want to have anything to do with that. Meanwhile, on the left is jungle, and protruding into the fairway from the left is a reed-filled marsh, which seems to be only 190-yards off the tee but is, in fact, 300-yards away (from the blue markers) and allows a full-blooded drive to be played by all but the best hitters. Many are fooled into going with an iron for safety and into hitting down the left for the same reason.

"Once on the fairway, the reeds dominate life: and the river on the right is still gnawing at the nerve-ends. The golfer who has played left off the tee is now faced with a second shot angled dangerously across the green towards the river! And it looks as though those reeds run all the way to the green and that a gigantic hit is required to carry them. In fact, the reeds run only from yard 300 to yard 405 and most golfers should have little bother in having their ball air-borne for those vital 105 yards on either their second or third shots . . . . and there is a bail-out area measuring 50-yards long by 100-yards wide between the reeds and the green. But only a portion of this bail-out zone is visible to the golfer and this helps to foster self-doubt as does the thought that a ball kept too far left will have to be played back towards the green at an angle that has the river behind the pin!"

"Another very important underlying principle of the design, as with all major courses, is that the handicap golfer is meant to use a handicap stroke to achieve a net par. But the silly and erroneous notion has got about that a handicap stroke is supposed to allow the golfer to achieve a net-birdie and scores from many clubs testify to the widespread official capitulation to this thinking."

In short, the European Club is a course for the cerebral golfer. But there are concessions to irrational thought, such as the famous *"Cursing Stone"* not far from the 10th tee.

According to the legend, you can curse a person or thing if you revolve the seven small stones on the top of the rock in an anti-clockwise direction. I would suggest that you will be having too much fun to be distracted by this but if your ego dominates your common sense, you may end up cursing your luck on this modern classic.

Top Ten Golf Courses in Ireland

Golf Digest July 2011

1. ***Royal County Down Golf Club***
   New Castle, County Down Links in the shadow of the Mourne Mountains on the edge of Dundrum Bay.
   www.royalcountydown.org

2. ***Portmarnock Golf Club***
   Portmarnock County Dublin. Internationally recognized as one of the top links courses in the world.
   www.portmarnockgolfclub.ie

3. ***Royal Portrush Golf Club***
   Portrush, County Antrim. Royal Portrush has been portrayed by many golfers as one of the most challenging courses in the world, requiring skill and concentration.
   www.royalportrushgolfclub.com

4. ***The European Club***
   Brittas Bay, County Wicklow. Consistently ranks among the top 100 courses in the world.

www.theeuropeanclub.com

5. *Ballybunion Golf Club*
   Ballybunion, County Kerry. One of the finest Links courses in the world. Golf Magazine rated 11th in the world.
   www.ballybuniongolfclub.ie

6. *Waterville House and Golf Links*
   Waterville, County Kerry. Mystical Links on the roaring Atlantic. Founded in 1889 and always in the top 10 in Ireland.
   www.watervillegolflinks.ie

7. *Lahinch Golf Club*
   Lahinch, County Clare. The Old Course is a classic links course with rolling dunes and fairways. The Castle course is an easier alternative.
   www.lahinchgolf.com

8. *Adare Manor Golf Club*
   Adare, County Limerick. Designed by Robert Trent Jones, signature hole #18 has been described as one of the finest Par 5's in the world.
   www.adaregolfclub.com

9. *County Louth Golf Club*
   Baltray, Drogheda, County Louth. One of the world's great links courses, and home to numerous major national and international championships.
   www.countylouthgolfclub.com

10. *Tralee Golf Club*

West Barrow, Ardfert, County Kerry. The Tralee Golf Club moved into the number 10 spot in 2010. Surrounded by the Atlantic, there are magnificent panoramic views from all holes. It was made famous in "Ryan's Daughter" in 1968.

www.traleegolfclub.com

Since all top golf courses are reviewed annually for ranking, go to **www.irishgolfdesk.com** for current rankings and visit each individual course website for detailed information on the desired course.

Marcus Treacy, a long time golfer living in Kilarney would add **Enniscrone www.enniscronegolf.com** and **Doonbeg www.doonbeglodge.com** to this list of famous Irish courses.

We would be remiss if the famed Palmer Ryder Cup Golf Course, **The K Club,** was not singled out as one of Europe's most spectacular golf courses. This course is ranked regularly in the top three parkland golf courses in Ireland, **www.kclub.ie/palmer-ryder-cup**

Hidden Gems

Throughout the island of Ireland, in both the Republic and Northern Ireland, there are dozens of fine golf courses, *Hidden Gems*, the so called "B" courses, out of the way, and relatively unknown except by the Irish. Sometimes referred to as "a course worth playing if you are in the area." You may want to include some of these jewels in your itinerary or build your golf tour entirely around these beautiful, inexpensive golf courses scattered throughout the island. Following are a few examples. Go on the web and search for others and you'll find images of these magnificent courses that you probably have never heard of, but will soon dream about playing. Following are a few in different regions of the island that we found by using the web and key words *hidden gems golf courses in Ireland.*

Connemara Golf Links in Ireland's northwest features uniquely rocky terrain that complements a region full of hidden gems that one can play for a fraction of the cost of better known golf courses like Lahinch or Tralee. For example, 18 holes of golf and a full Irish breakfast cost €37 at the start of the 2010 season. **www.connemaragolflinks. com**.

Ardglass Golf Club in County Down, Northern Ireland, north of New Castle is the one hidden gem links course you must play if your itinerary takes you north. A 13th Century castle ruin is the clubhouse and it is the oldest known structure used for that purpose. Unlike other links courses running along the sand dunes, the entire course sits on a rocky outcrop overlooking the sea at every turn. **www. ardglassgolfclub.com**

Ardglass Golf Club is situated on the Southeast coast of County Down. Ardglass is one of the most spectacular courses in Ireland. The course meanders its way out to the headland and then winds its way back home. The first five holes follow the sea and are truly memorable.

Photo Credit: Northern Ireland Tourist Board

Portumna Golf Club is located in the southeastern corner of County Galway in the very center of the Republic. It is a total escape from links golf along the coast with the 17th green at Portumna protected by water, sand and an impenetrable forest. This is a very local friendly course where members treat visitors as welcome guests and do not require that they empty their pockets to play. **www. portumnagolfclub.ie**.

There are other hidden gems besides golf courses in the island. At practically every turn in the road, you'll find something interesting you'll want to see, and many of these hidden gems are not in the guidebooks. *Ireland Hidden Gems–Lite* is a new iPhone app available as a free download from the following website or the app store at iTunes. The app is a "lite" version of this web site and features the ten top visitor attractions in many popular categories that are not found in guidebooks. **www.irelands-hidden-gems. com/iphone-app.html**

Coollattin Golf Club, Shillelagh, County Wicklow—This 18-hole parkland golf course is in a beautiful setting of mature redwood, oak, and beech woodlands that line the large fairways. **www.coollattingolfclub.com.**

Glen Cullen Golf Club, Dublin, County Dublin—This 9-hole parkland course has amazing views of Dublin Bay and is located next to Johnny Fox's Pub, the highest altitude pub (900 meters) in Ireland. **www.glencullengolfclub.com**

Bray Golf Club—Set on the side of Bray Head in County Wicklow, this relatively new course has excellent views of the mountains and coastal areas. Lush parkland settings make this course situated 30 minutes from Dublin City an excellent choice for a nearby challenge. **www. braygolfclub.com**

Stepaside Golf Course—Located on the Enniskerry Road on the south side of Dublin, this immaculate municipal course encounters heavy traffic during the summer months owing to its relatively inexpensive rates and the well-manicured course. Tricky to get to, somewhat easy to play, but a couple holes would challenge the best golfers. **www.stepasidegolfcourse.com**

Delgany Golf Club—Set further down the coast from Bray and slightly inland, this long and sloping parkland course offers challenging long and short holes for the average golfer. It also has the distinction of being the only course in Ireland where one plays the 17th hole before the 16th. A very long par 5 sweeps through a glen before straightening out for the view of the 19th hole . . . the bar! **www.delganygolfclub. com**

VII

SIGHTSEEING ON A GOLF TOUR IN IRELAND

"Did the sea define the land or the land the sea?
Each drew new meaning from the waves' collision
Sea broke on land to full identity"
Seamus Heaney

IT'S LIKELY THE primary goal for your tour to Ireland is to play as much golf on as many different courses as possible. However, it would be a loss if you didn't take the opportunity to discover your very own Ireland.

As stated in the preface, the purpose of this guide is to help you plan and prepare for your trip to Ireland. This section will advise you on where you can find detailed information on what to see and do in Ireland beyond playing golf. We purposely do not go into much detail about sightseeing in Ireland because many other resources are available to help you decide what is worth seeing. The Internet is the best source for current information and we have categorized dozens of great websites in the Appendix, making it easier for you to get all the information you need.

Rather than searching the Internet for countless individual sites without knowing which ones are the best, start by visiting Tourism Ireland's website, **www.tourismireland. com**. Tourism Ireland is the marketing body for both the Republic of Ireland and Northern Ireland. It was established under the framework of the Belfast Agreement of Good Friday 1998 and is jointly funded by both governments. It operates under the auspices of the North South Ministerial Council through the Department of Enterprise, Trade and Investment in Northern Ireland and the Department of Arts, Sport and Tourism in the Republic.

Tourism Ireland's website can provide you with almost everything you need to know about planning a vacation to Ireland. Their brochure entitled, "Your Very Own Ireland," which is available on request, provides an overview of what the island has to offer. With all this information, you will be able to plan a very exciting golf vacation. The following is an excerpt from the brochure:

Discover Your Very Own Ireland

Perched at the very edge of Europe, Ireland is a land apart. Almost impossibly romantic, it's criss-crossed with fuchsia-filled hedges and ringed by towering sea cliffs.

Ireland is dotted with prehistoric dolmens and divided by ancient mountain ranges. On a clear day from the top of the Macgillycuddy's Reeks in Kerry—Ireland's highest mountain range—you'll be able to see right across the Island, or watch the Atlantic Ocean perform its riotous party piece along dramatic coastlines. Of course, with the Atlantic so nearby, clear days can't be absolutely guaranteed. But then Ireland doesn't have the greenest scenery in the world by accident. Should your vacation coincide with a few 'fine soft days', don't fret—you can always join the inn crowd. Ireland boasts the finest pubs in the world where you might just experience the odd late night, joining conversations that sparkle and leap like electricity. Songs will be sung, and the cares of the day will melt away and seem as insubstantial as a Galway sea mist. An intoxicating combination of breathtaking landscape, color, light and moving waters has brought the cliffs of Moher, the Ring of Kerry and the Giants Causeway to the attention of the world. But 'undiscovered Ireland' also awaits you—in the tightly hedged drumlin fields of ancient Ulster, or in the quiet pastoral lands of Offaly or Tipperary.

Rambling through unspoilt countryside, there's time for contemplation in Ireland. Even better, tailor-made places exist specially for the job. If you manage to visit the likes of Clonmacnoise monastic ruins as the dying sun sinks beyond the sweep of the Shannon, you might contemplate on how this place helped shape the Christian world. Ireland is waiting to be discovered—no matter what your age or your background, here we believe that life holds an adventure for you. It might be an expedition along the Shannon-Erne waterways discovering hidden villages en route, or it could be wandering through the ancient streets of Galway—there is something for you waiting to be discovered.

You can have capital fun too! Belfast, glorying in its Victorian grandeur, has nooks and crannies enough to fill a book, Dublin with its Georgian elegance and contemporary élan is one of the most welcoming cities in the world, while Cork's ancient buildings and modern outlook are a constant source of surprise and delight.

Ireland is an ethereal place, a gentle place. It remains an oasis of charm and tireless beauty in an increasingly busy world. You can meditate amongst ancient friaries, or partake in the pagan abandon that are the country's festivals. The

Wicklow Gardens Festival, the Castleward Opera or the Bantry Mussel Fair are part of the fabric of the community, and you won't be there long before you enter into the spirit of things!

The individual character of towns and villages is a very special feature of Ireland—locally owned pubs; cafes and stores make shopping an enriching experience. International names are available, too—Waterford Crystal, Belleek China, Guinness or Bushmills whiskey all are renowned throughout the world. And even if you don't buy any souvenirs on your visit, your memories will ensure that you still take home treasures.

Here is a short list of some of the fascinating places on the Emerald Island you may want to visit. Of course you will have to plan accordingly around your golf schedule.

- *Bushmill's Distillery*, the world's oldest whiskey distillery in County Antrim, where a wonderful new museum and visitors' tour is now offered
- *The medieval banquets in the Shannon region* complemented by such wonderful attractions as the Bunratty Folk Park, where rural and urban life in 19th century Victorian Ireland is recreated
- *Glenveagh Castle and Gardens* in County Donegal, in the Northwestern corner of Ireland
- *King John's Castle,* an imposing 13th century fort in the heart of medieval Limerick
- *Craggaunowen*, a recreation illustrating the story of the Celts' arrival in Ireland
- *Challenge your golf game* on any of the 400 plus golf courses on the Island—from the world-famous Royal County Down and Lahinch to the lesser-known gems like Carne and Ballyliffin.

- *The grave of St. Patrick* in County Down dating from 461 A.D.
- Those natural-occurring *geological or topographical wonders* such as the Cliffs of Moher or The Burren, both in County Clare or the Giants' Causeway in County Antrim
- The many *art galleries and museums* throughout Ireland that showcase and commemorate the human talents of Irish artists in all forms of artistic endeavors, especially literature, sculpture and painting. The Crawford Municipal Art Gallery in Cork and the National Gallery of Ireland in Dublin, where you will also find the Writers Museum and the National Wax Museum
- Explore Ireland's number-one tourist attraction, *The Guinness Tour,* providing an unforgettable welcome and a magical journey deep into the heart of the world famous GUINNESS® brand and company. This historical building is central to Dublin's and Ireland's heritage, and has been continually updated to create a fascinating industrial tradition with a contemporary edge. *TIP:* If you're going to Dublin, plan ahead and get your tickets online and avoid the long queue when you get there. **www.Guinness-storehouse.com**
- *Culture and Theater*—Ireland is a country rich in arts, culture, festivals and theater. A cultural tour of Ireland will introduce you to literary giants such as Oscar Wilde and Jonathan Swift. On your tour you can experience listening and dancing to native music in rural and big city pubs where you will find musicians with local instruments playing to enthusiastic crowds. You can also experience

great theater at the Barabbas Theater Company in Dublin, the National Folk Theater in Kerry County, the Town Hall Theater in Galway and theatrical groups throughout the country

- *For more information on* Ireland and its festivals, theaters, woolen mills and activities for the none-golfer, check the Appendix at the end of this book, which lists dozens of great websites or visit **www.discoverireland.com**.

SW Ireland Killarney Base

- The Ring of Kerry, stunning mountain and coastal views (110 miles, but can be shortened)
- The Dingle Peninsula, small in size yet topographically diverse and scenic, long sandy beaches and pretty villages.
- Ride the old steam train between Tralee and Blennerville
- Gap of Dunloe (5 miles from Killarney) 15th Century Muckross Abbey and House

Shannon Base

- Cliffs of Moher (6 miles) and O'Brien's Tower, terrific ocean views over sheer cliffs that drop straight into the Atlantic
- Bunratty Castle (1425), one of Ireland's most authentic fortresses
- Doolin (10 miles), listen to traditional music in one of the town pubs
- Lisdoonvarna, a spa town famous for its matchmaking festival, stick close to your wife!

- The Burren, a lunar landscape full of wild flowers and animals
- The old-World Aran Islands

County Antrim

- Carrick-a-Rede Rope Bridge, Located on the North Antrim coast, this unique bridge is 70 ft long and hangs 80 ft above the ocean
- Dunluce Castle, Ruins of a late-medieval castle in the county Antrim
- Carrickfergus Castle, Norman castle on the shore of Belfast Lough
- Glenariff Forest Park, part of the famous nine 'Glens of Antrim' Glenariff is known as the 'Queen of the Glens' and is located in the county Antrim

County Down

- Silent Valley, a mountain park featuring the famous Mourne Wall
- Ulster Folk and Transport Museum, recently voted Irish museum of the year, it tells the story of life in Northern Ireland in the early 20th century.
- Exploris Aquarium, classic family fun filled with various sea creatures

County Armagh

- Armagh Planetarium, activities include rocket building, meteorite impacts, solar viewing and space robots.

- The Argory, beautiful Irish gentry house; a National Trust property

Northern Ireland

- Derry City or Londonderry, popular for shoppers and sightseers
- Belfast City, home to the Belfast Zoo
- Ulster American Folk Park, emphasis is on the emigration from Ulster to the USA. Experience the past firsthand, arriving in the 'New World'.

Great Golf and Scenery in Northwestern Ireland and Northern Ireland

Authors' note: The following discussion on Northern Ireland is presented with permission from its author, Sandy Glenn.

Americans typically head to the southwest of Ireland when seeking great links golf in Europe. But why stop there when the north offers so much?

The southwest of Ireland is very popular with American golfers for good reason. The weather is typically tamer, there is an abundance of well-known golf courses and there are lots of touristy towns and sites to keep a visitor busy during non-golf times.

An alternative that offers up some of the most spectacular and challenging links in the world is the northwest coast in The Republic of Ireland along with the coast of Northern Ireland. These parts are prolific with wild fairways and clever greens that simply beg the golf lover to give them a go.

Untamed Beauty in Northwest Ireland

Enniscrone Golf Club (**www.enniscronegolf.com**) is about a 45-minute drive from the village of Sligo located on the Northwest coast in Leitrim County. There are 18 stunning holes (visit this excellent web site for a virtual tour of all 18 holes) that roam throughout the towering dunes of the Enniscrone strand. Blind shots abound and slick, tricky greens keep you on your toes as you fight the elements of strong coastal winds. Greens fees are reasonable at about $45 US and they even offer up husband and wife specials. Two outstanding yet decidedly challenging courses are the Old Tom Morris Links (in play for over a century) and the new Sandy Hills Links at the Rosapenna Hotel & Golf Resort (**www.rosapenna.ie).** These links located between the very scenic Sheephaven and Mulroy Bay on the Rosguill Peninsula are set to become a top destination. The geography of this area, north of the large village of Letterkenny, is breathtaking. Walking this course is not for the faint of heart as the inclines are steep, but that is only part of the challenge. Narrow fairways protected by thick dunes grass make this target golf at its best. Wild winds and rain, should the weather act up, add to the multiple calculations of how to properly survive each hole.

Greens fees are free to Rosapenna Hotel guests and are very reasonable for non-guests at around $70 US. The Downings Bay Hotel, which is virtually just down the road, offers up a terrific deal that includes a low room rate (daily breakfast included and a dinner for two) plus two rounds of golf at Rosapenna.

Harbour Bar is a favorite 19th hole in the town of Downings Bay. Live, traditional Irish music is served up in this small, intimate setting where you can share some good craic with the locals.

The Country of Northern Ireland

This small country on the north of the Emerald Isle is a gem when it comes to beauty, scenery and golf. The Giant's Causeway coastline is stunning with its abundantly green pastures, sea views and historic sites. Dunluce Castle, Giant's Causeway, Carrick-A-Rede Rope Bridge and Bushmill's are all located within a small perimeter. The villages of Portrush and Portstewart make great bases for this area, especially when it comes to golf.

A standout is the *Portstewart Golf Club* **www. portstewartgc.co.uk,** particularly the front nine holes. A hugely elevated tee box above the fairway is the beginning of some amazing golf and could be the most dramatic opening hole to be found anywhere in the world. The Atlantic Ocean is to your right, the wind is blasting across the tee box, and rolling links are to your left. The course is one of the finest to be seen anywhere, although the last three finishing holes could be considered a bit disappointing as 16 heads straight to the clubhouse, 17 goes back out, then 18 comes back to the clubhouse yet again. Greens fees are around $120 US, which is fairly remarkable for such a dramatic, exhilarating course.

The courses discussed are but a wee taste of what Northwest Ireland and Northern Ireland have to offer. Use the Internet and this guide and begin to design a perfect golf getaway.

VIII

YANKEE GOLFERS IN IRELAND

"Even if the ball was wrapped in bacon, Lassie couldn't find it," as heard from an Irish caddie, after a particularly bad shot.

AMERICAN GOLFERS ENJOY a good reputation among the natives in Ireland. On a recent trip to Ireland, I (Bill Ruskin) asked caddies, proprietors, tour bus drivers, and *drinking consultants* their opinion of Yankee golfers in their country and to relate any interesting stories about them.

In the Hotels and Guest Houses

Aidan Teahan, the assistant manager of the Grand Hotel in Tralee says that, "American golfers exude confidence. Generally Americans are happier, more confident, and usually very polite. They are also mostly conservative. I've never seen an American go overboard in my hotel."

At the Brookhaven Guest House in Waterville, I spoke to the proprietor, Mary Clifford, who told me, "We love to have American golfers stay with us, and many do since Brookhaven Guest House is the only four-star guest house in Waterville. (**www.brookhavenhouse.com**) In fact, during this economic downturn, our doors would be closed if it wasn't for American golfers. I can tell you lots of stories about Americans. For example, it's not unusual for totally committed American golfers (primarily from the east coast) to pursue the following crazy golf itinerary:

Day 1. Arrive in Shannon and drive to Ballybunion, play one or even two rounds and then drive to Waterville and check into Brookhaven Guest House.

Day 2. Play two rounds at Waterville Links Course, then dinner, drinks, and back to Brookhaven for some sleep.

Day 3. Drive to Old Head and play two rounds, then drive back to Waterville for an overnight in the guesthouse.

Day 4. Drive to Shannon for the 1:30 pm flight back to the USA.

"While this schedule is stunning to us, the Yankee golfers are exhausted but happy and sleep all the way home. We love the enthusiasm and spirit of American golfers."

In The Pubs

Niall Hayles, who described himself as a 'Leprechaun on Steroids' and carries a business card identifying himself as a 'Drinking Consultant' was behind the bar at the popular Sean Og's Pub in Tralee. (**www.sean-ogs.com**)

He told me, "We see a lot of American golfers in this pub, especially since we have accommodations upstairs. They can enjoy live, traditional music six nights a week, drink until we close, then stagger up the stairs and fall in bed. They love it! Yanks frequently ask us to describe the various terms for the pub beer we sell."

A Pint is always a Guinness

A Pint of Beer is a Smithwicks

A Pint of Lager is any Irish Blonde

A Black and Tan is Guinness and Smithwicks

A Pint of Derry is a full pint of Smithwicks with a Guinness head

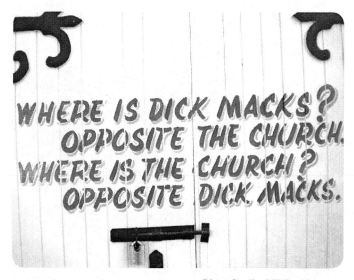

Photo Credit: Bill Ruskin

When ordering a drink in Irish pubs, remember most of them close at midnight. When it nears the closing time, don't be surprised to hear the owners start yelling, "Drink-up, drink-up!!"

Pub is short for public house. Go to an Irish pub even if you don't drink. We heard some wonderful stories in the pubs. It seems that every one of them has its central character: a well-defined Irish gentleman, who at sight of a fresh pint sitting in front of him, is ready to relate endless stories about golf and / or Irish life in general. Almost every pub character we met in the Dingle Peninsula told us that they had some part in the popular movie *Ryan's Daughter*, a 1970 movie filmed in the isolated village of Kirrary. While in Ireland, you must go into a pub in a small town, say hello, buy a round and spend an hour talking. When your journey to Ireland is over, the experiences in the pubs will be second in your memory only to the amazing golf you will have played. As Rick Steves says in his guide to Europe, "a pub is an extended living room where, if you don't mind the stickiness, you can feel the pulse of Ireland."

Dick Macks Pub in Dingle, County Kerry, rated as one of the best pubs in Ireland. At one time, it was a leather shop by day and a pub at night. A small leather shop is still on display in this happy watering hole that is greatly popular with locals and international visitors

Photo Credit: Bill Ruskin

In Sheilin's Seafood Restaurant in Waterville, we heard many golf stories from Michael Courtney who originally started the restaurant now managed by his family. Michael told us that Payne Stewart, who is revered in Ireland, loved Waterville and always carried a harmonica with him to play in the pubs he visited in Ireland.

In 1978 or '79 (as keen as Michael's memory was, he didn't know the exact year), Nick Faldo, who was playing on the Pan Am team, came into Sheilin's with his eye patched up. (He'd been practicing and one of his teammates whacked him with a ball.)

Waterville is famous for its Links Course and the Waterville House, where many of the professional golfers often stay while practicing for the open in the U.K. Tiger Woods is a frequent visitor there and it is a common sight to see him in the local restaurants.

Dublin and Guinness are synonymous, or almost. Equally important to meeting Irish people and playing golf, drinking a 'pint' in an Irish pub is a big part of the Irish Experience. (Once again, if you ask for a pint in an Irish pub you'll get a Guinness.) In September 2009, Guinness celebrated its 250th anniversary with events in Dublin and around the world. Here are some facts about Guinness that you may not know but will make your visit to the pub of your choice even more enjoyable because you'll know something about Guinness other than its great taste.

- In 1759, Arthur Guinness took a leap of faith and signed a lease that tied him to pay annual rent at St. James Street in Dublin of £45 for the next 9,000 years.
- Arthur Guinness's decision to turn a pastime into a profession had a long-term effect on Dublin,

providing employment, housing, sports facilities, public amenities and charitable foundations for its people.

- Within a hundred years of being set up, the Guinness brewery was the largest in Ireland. By 1886, it was the largest in the world.
- By 1900, it was estimated that one person in 30 in Dublin was dependent on Guinness for their livelihood.
- Generations of the Guinness family engaged in acts of philanthropy, which changed the shape and look of the city.
- When the barley is being roasted, the whole city smells of burnt toast or coffee or yeast. The brand accounts for 40% of the Irish pub trade, and indeed, despite the best efforts of other stouts, the words "pub" and "Guinness" seem to have an unbreakable association for many Irish people. You can enjoy red wine, lager, or a gin and tonic wherever you want. But for pints of Guinness, the thinking goes, you need to be in a pub.
- The characteristic smell of roasting barley will continue to be part of Dublin life and visitors to the city will keep trooping to the Guinness Storehouse where the cost of admission for four adults is roughly the same as the rent negotiated by Arthur Guinness 250 years ago.
- Arthur's Day takes place on 24 September, with concerts in St. James Gate and celebrations throughout Dublin. **www.guinness.com**

Guinness facts from an article article "The Right Stuff" by Chris Binchy published in CARA Magazine September 2009.

On the Links

A caddie at Tralee shared his thoughts, saying, "Most American golfers are in Ireland at considerable expense and out to enjoy themselves in the pubs and golf courses. I find them generally well behaved. Some think they are better golfers than they are. In particular, they are not used to Links courses and it takes a couple of rounds for them to adjust.

"American golfers should come in May or September; we have better weather then and cheaper rates. Also, tell them to bring plenty of golf balls. You can never bring too many and you can always leave any extras with your caddie. I would recommend the golfer bring at least one Rescue Wood (Loft 21°-23°). These clubs seem to help Americans on the Links."

Fergal, a caddie at Tralee Golf Club who doesn't remember how long he has been a caddie said that, in general, American golfers are enjoyable to be with and very welcome at Tralee, "but don't take the recession out on the caddie," he pleaded.

Generally it's one caddie per bag. He did caution that you couldn't reserve or guarantee caddies, only request them. That is why it's best to plan ahead and get your request to the club well in advance.

- Fee's for Junior Caddies are: €25-30/bag + tip
- For a Senior Caddy: €35-40/bag + tip

American golfers planning to go to Ireland can shop around for the bargain prices if your party hasn't decided which courses they want to play. There will be plenty of bargains ahead and special offers are advertised in local newspapers all the time (*see Appendix for newspaper websites*). For example, the K-Club in Dublin, the venue for the 2007 Ryder Club (**www.kclub.ie**), was offering two rounds of golf, two nights at a B&B and dinner for just €250 through newspaper ads in September 2010.

Be prepared for four seasons

One caddie I met in a pub offered up his suggestions; "American golfers should be prepared for 'four seasons' in one round of golf. Bring your weather proofs. Generally Americans are on time for tee times and have a good, positive attitude with minimal complaints. I would recommend that the American golfer take an extra club on all shots due to distance and wind conditions."

Yankee Golfers like Irish beer

Tour bus drivers have continuous exposure to American golfers and they overhear a lot from Americans about golfing in Scotland and Ireland. I talked with John Fleming, a driver of a van with J. O'Callaghan and Son Luxury Transport Service (**www.jocgroup.com**). He was waiting in the parking lot for his golfing party to return from a links course. His group had recently played in Scotland and was now playing several courses in Ireland. He told me, "Most American golfers behave well while playing in both Ireland and Scotland (it is easy to go back and forth with the excellent ferry system). The only problem is when they drink too much in the pubs and then carry on in the hotels. The majority of American golfers are orderly and well behaved.

"I hear from the golfers that most of them prefer to play golf in Ireland," he said, "they like the green color of the island, and the pubs are great. In fact, the golfers like the pubs almost as much as the golf. They also like the friendly Irish people."

'Le pree shuns' on the golf courses

Martin Troy, an Irish expatriate from Shankill, County Dublin, lives in Colorado Springs and is Assistant Manager of Jack Quinn's Irish Pub & Restaurant. While living in Ireland, Martin was a senior bartender for the Porter House Pub in Bray and met many Yankee golfers when they stopped in after playing rounds at Royal Portrush in Northern Ireland and the likes of Druids Glen, Donabate, Portmarnock, Woodbrook and many others.

Martin was working one day in the Porter House Pub when a large group of Germans came in, followed by two American couples. Soon after, one of the bartenders barged into his office and said, "Martin, there is an American woman out there with a strange request. She wants to know if there are any 'le pree shuns' on the golf courses around here and if she could buy one."

Scratching his head, Martin went out and talked with the lady and discovered that she was looking for Leprechauns. She actually thought she could buy a Leprechaun in a pub. "Someone was winding her up with a prank and she fell for it hook, line and sinker," Martin said. Then he decided it was time to explain to her that "a Leprechaun is just a mischievous elf of Irish folklore and none have ever been seen playing golf around Dublin, at least not with a respectable score."

Start on one course—finish on another!

A group of Asian golfers once teed off at County Louth (Baltray) and ended up finishing their round on neighbouring Seapoint. They had inadvertently crossed the boundary wall when heading for the 14th tee and continued their game on the fine links next door. They didn't realize their mistake until they headed to the car park to search, in vain, for their hire car but were soon fed and watered and taken back to Baltray, where they picked up their car and continued their journey.

American golfers have yet to make the same mistake as far as anyone knows, buy they are always welcome visitors, despite what you might have heard.

A thorn in the side of the tour guide

One story, probably specious, concerns a group of Americans on tour. They were accompanied by a particularly grouchy woman, who became a thorn in the side of the tour guide because of her constant complaining. When they arrived in Cork to visit the Blarney Stone, which they say grants lifelong good luck to anyone who kisses it, the guide feared the worst when he discovered that the tourist attraction was closed for the day. "Perhaps we can come back tomorrow," the guide ventured, triggering a torrent of abuse from the woman. "Well now," the guide said, "it is said that if you kiss someone who has kissed the stone, you'll have the same good fortune."

"And I suppose you've kissed the stone," the woman sneered.

"No, ma'am," the guide replied with a twinkle in his eye, "but I've sat on it."

Fishing

Ireland is a fishing mecca for salmon and sea trout. If you feel the urge to add fishing to your itinerary, you are in the right country. Some Americans will fish using a 'ghillie' or a fishing guide; others will hire a boat and engine to go on their own. All you will need to bring is money for rental gear and a fishing license, which can be secured at any local tackle shop. Waterville is very popular for golfers desiring a combination of amazing links golf and great fishing.

"Luck of the Irish" is with a Yankee Golfer on Waterville's 7th

In 2002, Jim Hayes, Member 67 of the Old Head Golf Club, contacted his golfing buddy James Larkin, a notable Irish writer, editor and golfer from Dublin to help organize a golf tour for seven Yankee golfers from Colorado Springs. Stuart Scott was a last minute fill-in and all golfers in the two foursomes, except Scott and Steve Suggs, had a hole-in-one at one time or another in their golf life.

From the very beginning of the tour, it became routine at the pubs or dinner tables for someone to ask the question, "who at this table has not had a hole in one?" Scott and Suggs would reluctantly raise their hands.

On the infamous day that brought a new set of values to Scott's golfing life, he woke up not feeling well, so he bought a giant can of Guinness trusting it would settle him down. Like his stomach, the weather wasn't cooperating either, raining and with a strong wind, a normal gloomy golfing day. "Gloomy?? Hell no it was a glorious day . . . I'm in Ireland," Scott thought to himself at the time.

In 2002, the 7th at Waterville was the Bog Hole, a par 3, 139 yards from the green tee box. (In 2004 Tom Fazio completed a two-year re-model of the Waterville Links including the 7th that is now a par 4 named Teacher). Scott decided to use a pitching wedge but as he walked to the tee, his caddie said, "It's a nine iron." Wisely taking the caddie's advice and changing clubs, Scott put his stomach and the wind, rain and mist out of his mind and took his best swing at the Bog Hole pin.

"It's in the hole," yelled Jim Hayes, as the ball hit the green and they watched as the ball bounced, rolled to the left and went into the cup. Although excited for Scott, Ray Deeny, another golfer in the group, groaned at the prospect of losing another bet.

When Scott tells the story of his hole-in-one, he recalls to the best of his memory, that as they approached the hole to retrieve the ball from the cup, a figure came out of the mist dressed in a wool cap and a dark coat, introduced himself as Liam Higgins, and with a strong Irish accent asked Scott, "Would ye like me to attest to your hole-in-one, laddie?" Then Scott adds in a small disclaimer that the Guinness he had been drinking may have influenced his recollection of the exact event that occurred. You see, Liam Higgins is an Irish golfer who in 1973 crushed a drive 360 yards on the 16th and put the ball onto the green and into the hole. This shot was remarkable since the 16th is a big sweeping crescent shape and the flight path of Liam's ball followed the crescent and over a "mountain" in the middle of the turn. The hole was subsequently named after him and is now called *Liam's Ace*. Liam was the former head professional at Waterville and he now has the designation of Waterville's "touring professional" and holds the course record of 62. His son Brian, is Director of Golf at Waterville.

Following the round, and after everyone in sight learned about the Yank who made a hole-in-one on the 7th, the golfers returned to the Waterville Club House. There, Scott continued to broadcast his hole-in-one to anyone who would listen and ordered drinks on him for everyone in the pub. When the other foursome including Suggs came into the pub, they all sat down together. After a round was ordered and a toast was made to Scott, someone asked, "Who among us has not had a hole-in-one?" Suggs raised his hand. Scott didn't, and Suggs then realized he was now a minority of one.

When the celebrating was over and the tab came, Scott did the unthinkable in an Irish Pub by leaving a tip large enough, as he proudly quips, "to round off the tab to an even $100, which equaled my score for the round with the hole-in-one." To this day, Scott still carries the scorecard (now laminated) and the pub bill around in a special case showing it to anyone who cares to listen to the story.

The saga of his hole-in-one continued after the golfers left the pub and headed back to Kenmare where they were staying. Still wound up from the golf shot that earlier he'd only dreamt about making, Scott announced that he was buying dinner, but everyone was going to have traditional Irish stew to celebrate. The group agreed to that deal and Hayes called ahead to the Lime Tree restaurant in Kenmare to reserve Irish stew for seven hungry golfers.

"We only make Irish Stew in the winter," came the reply. So the story of Scott's hole-in-one was repeated for the 14th time on the phone and when the golfers arrived at the Lime Tree restaurant, beautiful bowls of fresh Irish stew were ready for them. A great finish to a great day!

As a final note to this story, whenever these Yankee golfers get together to play or have a beer, the question always comes up, "who among us has never had a hole in one?" Suggs is the only one to raise his hand, but now looks at Scott and says, "Sure, you've had a hole in one, but you've never had a birdie!"

Authors note: According to Brian Higgins, his father Liam set the course record of 62 the day he aced the 16th. That was the course record off the white markers until Tony Jacklin set the course record of 61 off the blue tees. But these scores were before the Fazio changes. As a course record should be recorded during tournament play, John B. O'Shea holds the new record off the white markers at 67. There hasn't been a tournament using back tees since the changes, so the Jacklin record still stands.

A great 5-iron hit

One of Tralee's famous caddies, Chucky O'Connell, was caddying for an American golfer. On the 16th hole, the man wanted to hit a 6 iron but Chucky insisted he needed a 5 iron. Eventually the man took Chucky's advice but he wasn't convinced. He proceeded to hit a beautiful 5 iron, except the ball was still rising as it flew over the green and out-of-bounds. Chucky came straight over, shook the man's hand and said, "May I congratulate you, sir. You are one of the best 5-iron hitters I have ever seen."

A Misunderstanding in a Belfast Pub

As a bartender in a popular Irish pub, Martin Troy met a lot of Yankee golfers. A group of about 10 marketing executives on a corporate junket with an open expense account came into the Porter House pub and related an event that happened to them in Belfast. After playing at the Royal Portrush Golf Club, the golfers went back to the Royal Court Hotel Portrush for some drinks.

One of the golfers innocently asked the bartender if he could make a "car bomb." (A car bomb is a legitimate drink consisting of a one-half glass of Guinness, a shot of coffee liquor and Irish Cream). For whatever reason, the bartender on duty didn't know about this drink, took offense and asked the Yankee golfers to leave the establishment. Understandably, the implication is a very sensitive issue in Northern Ireland.

Discussion of the misunderstanding ensued, and in the end, no feelings were hurt and everyone was congenial. As the evening wore on, the Yanks shared a few pints with the bartender and left a substantial tip, even though tipping in pubs is not usually encouraged.

It's worth noting that some Americans have the impression that Northern Ireland is still in turmoil after having been through a very emotional and violent time. The conflict is over. The people of Northern Ireland are most hospitable and welcome visitors to the beautiful northern part of the island. Belfast is a safe city to visit, offering great music including native instruments in pubs, jazz and blues concerts and many cultural and art events. Some of the most ornately decorated pubs on the island can be found in Belfast, such as Robinsons, an old traditional Victorian pub and the Crown Liquor Saloon with beautiful stained glass booths.

FAQ's

An American golfer asked a farmer why his sheep grazing on the hill are painted different colors.

The farmer replied, "Wool from the red colored sheep is for blankets and wool from the blue-colored sheep is for sweaters, scarves, and gloves."

"How do you know what color to paint each sheep?" the golfer asked.

The farmer replied, "You feel underneath the sheep and then you know what color to use."*

David Power, head professional at Tralee, told us that surprisingly, American golfers often ask, "Can you get a drink at the bar? The humored response from us is always, "Well, that is probably the best place." He also related that they get golfers in the pro shop who proceed to ask, "Is this the pro shop?" Again, he finds this very funny.

There's a castle by the third hole at Tralee. Two Americans were playing there and they asked the caddie, "How old is that castle?" The caddie replied, "It's 814 years and 3 months." The Americans were astounded at the age of the castle and equally amazed at the caddie's very exact answer. Their curiosity got the better of them and they asked, "How can you be so accurate about the age?" The caddie replied, "Well when I first came here, they told me it was 800 years old and I have been caddying for 14 years and 3 months."

---

* This joke is based on the arcane knowledge that sheep farmers in Ireland mark their animals with colors that identify their gender, not the suitability of their wool for different items of clothing. Like most local jokes, it pokes fun at strangers who are both unfamiliar with unique customs and unwilling to wait and watch until they figure out the puzzle.

IX.

PLANNING YOUR TRAVEL TO IRELAND

"Twenty years from now, you will be more disappointed by the things that you didn't do than by the ones you did do. So throw off the bowlines. Sail away from the safe harbor. Catch the trade winds in your sails. Explore. Dream. Discover."

Mark Twain

WE TRUST WE'VE been successful in the introduction and preceding chapters of this guide to help convince you to go ahead and check off a golf tour to Ireland from your bucket list. Following are some helpful tips to successfully plan the all-important travel to your destination.

Minimum Length of Trip

- Plan on one travel day to Ireland (overnight flight), and one travel day to return to the USA. We suggest a minimum of six full days in Ireland for golf and to capture the Irish Experience. (If time allows, travelers from the western U.S. may consider breaking their first day with an overnight in their departure city, thus making the transatlantic leg less taxing.) You may want a day "off" from golf to soak up the culture and see the sights, as well.

- Confirm your flights with the airline 72 and 24 hours prior to departure.
- Check in at the airport two hours prior to departure and be sure to have with you:
  - Passports (travel with a photocopy of your passport, it will help if you happen to lose the original).
  - Properly identified baggage within weight limits.
  - Driver's license and golf handicap card
- Keep credit cards and currency on your person. A belt fanny pack works for some travelers. When you arrive, secure your passport in the hotel since you won't need it until you return to the USA.

Baggage Information

- Be certain to contact your airline for check-in times, carry-on and checked baggage restrictions. Ask if your specific style golf travel bag is acceptable.
- Know that you will probably have to pay for each checked bag. To Europe the cost could be as high as $50 per bag. Ask your airline to determine the actual cost because it varies. For example, Aer Lingus allows the first bag at no charge. Label all luggage with your name and the address of your first hotel in Ireland.
- Security procedures require all bags to be unlocked at check in

Regarding security, advancing technology and industry software for x-ray equipment changed the rules for carry on baggage in 2009. Check with your airline or go to **www. tsa.gov** for information on the rules regarding taking water, soft drinks, shampoos, and other liquids through security checkpoints.

- Normally you can check two pieces of luggage, not to exceed (note that airlines differ, this is an example):
    - Bag 1-62 inches and up to 70 pounds (L+W+H = inch value)
    - Bag 2-55 inches and up to 70 pounds
- Golf bags count as one piece of luggage and must be checked. They may have to be taken to a separate check in location.
- Carry on bags come in a variety of sizes. The standard for carry on baggage is one bag (22"x 14"x 9") with a total of 45" that must fit in the overhead bin or under the seat in front of you. You may also carry on one personal bag such as a handbag or small backpack. A laptop counts as a carry on if it is in a separate bag. Make sure to purchase a good piece of luggage that will withstand the abuse associated with modern travel.

Shopping For Airline Tickets

Hundreds of articles have been published on the subject of "getting the best airline ticket deals." Everyone who travels has their favorite travel website, whether it's Orbitz. com, Travelocity.com, or any of the numerous other travel websites.

We recommend that you do your shopping for the best deals on a Monday, Tuesday, or Wednesday, when airlines have the least demand for tickets. Your best travel days and times are usually Tuesday, Wednesday and Saturday afternoons. For detailed information on "how to land the best deals on airline tickets" and to learn about "The 10 rules of the road for air travel," visit **www.wsj.com** or write to Scott McCartney at **Middleseat@wsj.com**.

The Wall Street Journal Guide to Power Travel: How to Arrive with Your Dignity, Sanity, and Wallet Intact is a must have book for anyone who travels. Whether you are planning a golf trip to Ireland or a business trip to another state, this book by Scott McCartney, travel columnist for the Wall Street Journal, is your one-stop guide for no fuss, no muss travel. It has all the insider tips on how to:

- Find the lowest fares
- Decipher whether packages are good deals
- Find cheap rates at nice hotels
- Learn how to benefit when airlines cut rates after you buy
- Learn how to finagle lower baggage fees and upgrades and much more.

Also, McCartney's *2011 Stranded Fliers Survival Guide* discusses options on how to survive if you are stranded at an airport, including how to get a cot, food and the fastest flight out. Scott discusses how airports get turned into hotels and offers other strategies for stranded fliers.

For more travel rules, listen to a podcast with McCartney, or watch a *Power Travel* video with tips on making sure your luggage doesn't get lost at **www.online.wsj.com/public/page/news-travel-vacation.html**.

Recently the "vertical" travel search sites Kayak.com and Sidestep.com have merged. The new site, **www.kayak.com**, provides comparative travel cost information. With this merger, the companies have become the fifth largest travel site on the web and a powerful force in the Internet travel business as a whole. Kayak is a "meta" site, meaning it pulls data from other travel websites and make it available to customers in one place. This capability is especially helpful to International travelers because it will help various travel partners coordinate their plans.

Ireland Customs Allowances

This is what you can take with you:

- *From the USA to Ireland*: Travelers over the age of 17 may bring with them 200 cigarettes or 50 cigars, 1 liter of spirits over 22 proof, and 2 liters of fortified wine.
- *From Ireland to the USA*: Check with your airline for allowances on return, better yet, visit **www.uscustoms.com** for USA Custom information before you travel.

Airports in Ireland

Three main airports serve Ireland and Northern Ireland: Dublin Airport, Shannon Airport, and Belfast International Airport. Depending on your golf and ground itinerary, you may want to fly into one airport and leave from another.

Plan well in advance and coordinate arrival and departure times with your travel companions.

Dublin Airport—Serves flights from Boston, Atlanta, Los Angeles, Chicago, Newark, Philadelphia, Orlando and New York.

Shannon Airport—Serves flights from Atlanta, Boston, Chicago, New York, Newark and Philadelphia.

Belfast International-Serves flights from Newark only.

Check with your travel agent or directly with your preferred airline for other possible departure locations. To find information on airports, including arrivals and departures, parking, maps and facility guides, go to your preferred search engine and enter *airports in Ireland* and you will find links to all the airport information you will need for both Ireland and Northern Ireland.

Approximate flight times from some departure points in the USA:

AMERICAN CITIES	SHANNON
Boston	6.0 hours
New York	6.5 hours
Philadelphia	6.7 hours
Chicago	7.1 hours
Atlanta	7.7 hours
Denver	8.7 hours
Seattle	9.5 hours
Los Angeles	10.3 hours
San Francisco	10.4 hours

Transferring between London and Shannon, Ireland:

Flying ....approximately 1.25 hours
Driving/Ferry ....approximately 11.0 hours

TIPS: Driving from London to Ireland should be the absolutely last option unless you're planning several days for sightseeing along the way. If your itinerary takes you first to London, with a connecting flight on to Ireland, plan on waiting at least two hours between your arrival in London and your departure to your final destination.

Contact Information

Airlines	Telephone in USA/Ireland/website
American Airlines	800-433-7300
	01 602 0550
	www.americanairlines.com
Air Canada	888-247-2262
	01 661 0752
	www.aircanada.com
Aer Lingus	800-474-7424
	0818 365 0000
	www.aerlingus.com
British Airways	800-247-9297
	1890 626 747
	www.britishairways.com

Continental Airlines   800-523-3273
                       1890 925 252
                       www.continental.com

Delta Airlines   800-221-1212
                       1850 882 031
                       www.delta.com

Iceland Air   800-223-5500
                       84 4 811 1190
                       www.icelandair.co.uk

United Airlines   800-241-6522
                       (0) 845-8444-777 (in the UK)
                       www.united.com

Airports	**Telephone in USA / Ireland**
Shannon Airport	353 (0) 712000
Dublin Airport	353 (0) 1 814 1111
Belfast International Airport	44 (0) 28 9448 4848

Trip Protection Insurance

Because you are investing a great deal of time and hard earned money in this golf tour to Ireland, the uncertainty connected with international travel means that we highly recommend trip protection insurance to protect your investment.

Travel Guard, **www.travelguard.com** (800-826-1300) offers several plans that are customizable for golf travelers. The company's *Tee, Tour and Travel Plan* includes coverage such as trip cancellation, interruption, delay due to a covered reason, and medical expenses. In addition, the *Tee, Tour* *and Travel Plan* offers coverage unique to traveling golfers, including golf fee reimbursement due to course closure and coverage for golf equipment and/or baggage delay. Travel Guard will even reimburse a bar tab up to $250 for a golfer fortunate enough to score *a hole in one,* as long as it is witnessed and documented. The *Tee, Tour and Travel Plan* allows the traveler to purchase basic coverage up to 24 hours prior to departure, which includes:

- Trip cancellation (up to the trip cost) and interruption (up to 150% of the trip cost)
- Lost, stolen, or damaged baggage and travel documents (up to $2,500) ·
- Travel delay ($150 per day with a $1,500 maximum)·
- Baggage delay (up to $1,500.)
- Medical expense (up to $25,000)
- Medical evacuation (up to $500,000)

Also included are Livetravel® assistance (24/7 information hotline); 24/7 medical assistance; Bag Trak® luggage tracking; and special golf concierge services. These include golf club retrieval, assistance with golf club pickup, delivery and shipping (service only, customer responsible for fees), rental club reservations, assistance with ground transportation (limousines, shuttle buses, car rentals), event ticketing assistance for PGA, LPGA, and Senior PGA events, and restaurant referrals and reservations. Depending on your selection, other travel insurance plans available to golfers through Travel Guard can include:

- Fee Cost: Golf Course Closure

- Reimbursement for non-refundable golf fees if a golf course on your itinerary is closed due to inclement weather and you are given less than 24 hours notice of such closure.
- $1500: Trip Delay
- $250: Missed connection
- $750: Golf Equipment Delay
- Reimbursement for replacing essential items if your bags are delayed for more than 12 hours.
- $500,000: Emergency Evacuation and Repatriation of Remains—covers evacuation and transportation to the nearest adequate medical facility or home.

Many travel insurance plans through Travel Guard include additional benefits when you purchase your plan within 7 to 15 days after you initially purchase your tickets. These include coverage due to a financial default and a pre-existing medical condition exclusion waiver. To avoid surprises, know exactly what is in the travel insurance program you are buying. Don't assume you are covered for anything unless it is actually written in the program's Description of Coverage.

DISCLAIMER: This is only a brief description of the coverage(s) and assistance services available under the insurance programs available through Travel Guard. The Policy will contain reductions, limitations, exclusions and termination provisions. Insurance underwritten by National Union Fire Insurance Company of Pittsburgh, Pa., with its principal place of business in New York, NY. Coverage may not be available in all states. Travel assistance services provided by Travel Guard.

X.

WHAT TO TAKE: A Checklist for Packing

"You'll never meet a traveler who, after five trips, brags: "Every year I pack heavier." The measure of good travelers is how light they travel. You can't travel heavy, happy and cheap. Pick two."

Rick Steves

PACKING IS AN art that is especially practical for overseas trips where traveling as light as possible reduces the hassle. For insight into how seasoned travelers pack, visit **www.1000tips4trips.com** for over 1,000 travel tips submitted by international travelers.

Dress Code according to Brian Keogh

Unfortunately, the Irish are not known for sartorial elegance and golfing garb is particularly poor—think gardening clothes and you get the picture. Despite this, there is a strict dress code at all clubs and it is worth noting before you pack your bags to avoid any unnecessary embarrassment for you or your hosts.

Proper golf shoes are a must. Tennis shoes, trainers, hiking boots, or sandals are absolute no-nos. Most clubs now ban metal spikes. If you use metal, make sure you change to soft or plastic spikes before you travel. While many of the bigger clubs will replace your metal spikes with plastic "soft" spikes free of charge, this is not always possible at many of the smaller clubs.

Collared shirts or polo shirts must be worn, which means that you will not get away with a New York Jets shirt, an LA Lakers top or even an Irish rugby jersey.

Pants/trousers. Stay away from jeans, tracksuit bottoms (shell suits), and cargo pants with large pockets. If you are lucky enough to play on a sunny day and feel like playing in shorts, make sure they are tailored and not sports shorts, beach shorts or cut-offs. Many clubs insists that socks should be either knee-length (in any color) or white and ankle-length if shorts are worn.

Socks and trousers. Trousers must never be tucked into socks, unless you have just arrived at the club on a bicycle. Even then you will be expected to remove your trousers from your socks. If you really want to protect the ends of your trousers from mud, and you have the guts to wear them, opt for a pair of plus twos or plus fours (in America, they're called "knickers," which means another entirely different item of clothing in Ireland). Unless you can swing the club like Max Faulkner or the late Payne Stewart, this mode of dress is not recommended.

What to Pack—Ireland Isn't Mars, But . . .

Even if you've never been to Ireland before, it's unlikely you are expecting to walk onto the set of The Quiet Man with a golf club in your hand. Barring a fancy dress party, you are unlikely to bump into any black-clad widows or flame-haired youngsters leading a donkey and cart, piled high with peat.

Despite the demise of the financial whirlwind that was once known as the "Celtic Tiger," you will be able to buy almost everything essential for your trip in Ireland, except biscuits and gravy for breakfast* or root beer to quench your thirst after a long day on the golf course.

Packing for a foreign trip is something of an art form and it's always a good idea to make a list of those things you simply can't do without for a week or two.

Prescription medicines? Check. Reading glasses? Check. Travel insurance? Check. Bank cards/credit cards/traveler's cheques? Yes, these are all vital. But what about the basics, such as footwear, clothing and golf equipment?

Ireland has what is described as a temperate, maritime climate due to the presence of the Atlantic Ocean and the Gulf Stream. This is a fancy way of saying that it *rains all the time*, especially in summer when you are dying to get out and play a few holes. Winters are mild by comparison with those experienced by residents of the northern United States and the average daily temperature in winter varies from 4.0 °C (39.2 °F) to 7.6 °C (45.7 °F).

Irish people like to complain about the terrible summer weather, when temperatures vary from 12.3 °C (54.1 °F) to 15.7 °C (60.3 °F). But don't let those miserable summer temperatures put you off because they're perfect for golf.

---

* *In Ireland and the UK, the word "biscuit" is used for what Americans call crackers and cookies. Thus, biscuits and gravy would not be a very suitable replacement for a traditional Irish breakfast, which you are likely to find very much to your liking as fuel for a great day of golf.*

Not only that, it's the rain that makes Ireland so green, so we can't really complain.

What to Take For Your Golf Holiday

- *Trousers and sweaters.* You might be used to playing golf in balmy conditions back home but in Ireland, you are unlikely to need your shorts. It's amazing how cool it can become when the wind starts to blow, so pack a few sweaters just in case you need one coming down the last few holes on an overcast evening. Even if you don't need a sweater on the golf course, summer evenings can be cool as you sit on the club veranda sipping a pint of Guinness.

- If you have room in your luggage and can afford to pay for excess baggage, pack *two pairs of golf shoes.* Summer downpours are common and if you are planning to play golf daily, you will be glad to have that fresh pair of spare spikes and semi dry shoes the day after a wet round.

- Don't forget your *waterproofs.* And that's waterproof, not water resistant. Nick Faldo did himself no favours with the Welsh tourism authorities when he told the world to bring their Gore-Tex to the 2010 Ryder Cup at Celtic Manor. They were fortunate to get the matches finished by Monday. Wales and Ireland have similar climates, so don't say you weren't warned.

- In fact, it might not be a bad idea to bring a knitted hat (we call it a wooly hat) as well as a baseball cap. It can get chilly on those windy links courses, especially on an Irish summer's day, and nothing helps retain body heat as well as a good, old-fashioned wooly hat.

Whatever you do, always assume that it is about to rain. If the day stays fine, you might grumble about having to carry your waterproofs and your umbrella but if it turns nasty, you'll be glad you didn't put any faith in those watery, rays of sunshine you spied through the bedroom window before heading down for breakfast.

- The wind is always a factor and even if it is sunny, a chill northwest breeze is colder than you think. Invest in a *windcheater*, which you can wear under your sweater to keep the wind at bay. It's amazing the difference it makes. As the day warms up, you may find that you are too hot as you stride around the links. This is why most Irish golfers dress in more layers than an onion. Rather than wearing a thick sweater under your waterproof jacket or your windcheater, wear a couple of light sweaters instead, so you can peel off a layer if you become too warm.

- Needless to say, an *umbrella* and plenty of spare golf gloves are essential items. Bring plenty of golf balls with you as they are considerably more expensive in Ireland than the US.

- Bring a *light golf bag*. While you can rent clubs at most of Ireland's top courses, you'll enjoy your game even more if you bring your own sticks. But be warned; while they are becoming more common, not all Irish courses have golf carts. If you decide to hire a caddie, you won't have to worry about lugging your clubs up and down sand dunes searching for those wild drives. Even if you are a very straight hitter, your bagman will appreciate it if you leave that large golf bag at home. If you don't already own one, buy a pencil bag or a light bag with a pop-up stand. Not only will it make it easier to negotiate your way around airports, it will be far less tiring to tote around.

- *Sunscreen.* Okay, we don't get that much sunshine in Ireland but it is amazing how easily you can get burnt to a crisp, even on a cloudy day. Windburn is also a major hazard so make sure you pack plenty of sunscreen and avoid the beetroot look and long-term health risks associated with extreme exposure to the elements.

- Your *passport* is a must but if you plan to drive in Ireland, don't forget your driver's license from home, as it will be impossible to rent a car without one. Make sure it is hasn't expired.

- *Visas.* You will need your passport, of course, but US visitors do not need a visa for tourist or business stays of up to three months. Visit the Embassy of Ireland website for the most current visa information. You may also contact the Irish Embassy at 2234 Massachusetts Avenue, NW, Washington, DC 20008, tel: 1-202-462-3939, or the Irish consulate nearest you; these are located in Boston, Chicago, New York, and San Francisco.

- *Money.* Ireland is a member of the European Union and the Euro zone, which means that you will need Euros in your wallet. The good news is that if you are travelling to another Euro zone country following your Irish trip, you won't have to change currency. There are 16 countries in the Euro zone, including France, Germany, Spain, Italy, the Netherlands and Greece. Northern Ireland is part of the United Kingdom and uses the pound sterling as its currency, not the Euro.

Other Helpful Bits of Information

- *Power:* You will need a power adapter if you bring your American electrical appliances to Ireland (i.e. laptop, cell phone charger, iPad, etc.). All electrical sockets are three-prong, 220 watts, the same as the UK. You should have no problem buying one at most discount stores or even in airports (if you forget to get one earlier!).

- *Play all day (almost):* There's one big advantage to living on a small island on the far western edge of Europe, the summer days are long. At the height of the season, it's light by 6.30 am and doesn't get dark until after 11 pm, which means that playing 36 holes in a day shouldn't be a big problem.

- *Tipping:* This is something of an art form in Ireland and nowhere near as common as it is in the US. A tip of 10 or 15 percent is normal in restaurants, unless the bill (check) says, "service charge Included." Tipping in pubs is not common. You can tell the barman to "have one for yourself," though many people will leave change for table service in the lounge.

Essential Golf Equipment/Clothing (check list)

- ❏ Golf clubs / travel bag or case
- ❏ Two pairs of golf shoes (waterproof if possible)
- ❏ Two pairs of rain gloves
- ❏ Minimum three dozen golf balls, extra tees (note: golf balls can be expensive if you have to buy them in the pro shop just before you tee off) On the Internet, we found Titleist Pro V1's for €47/£42

per dozen in Ireland which is about $67, compared to Dick's Sporting Goods at around $40 per dozen. Any extra balls you don't use or lose can be given away as a friendly gesture.

❑ Rain cover for golf bag
❑ Top quality rain gear—waterproof/windproof jacket and pants (Gore-Tex is the best, don't skimp with poor quality rain gear).
❑ Three golf shirts with collar—wrinkle free
❑ One sweater, one sweatshirt or turtleneck and a wooly sailors cap since your regular golf cap will likely blow away. If you don't have one, you may want to wait and buy a logo cap at a golf club in Ireland. It will be a nice souvenir.
❑ Extra socks
❑ Two pairs of slacks, wrinkle free, washable and quick drying and good quality
❑ One warm, wind proof jacket

Miscellaneous

❑ Personal items/ toiletries
❑ Point-and-shoot camera, notebook, pens, addresses for postcards **Tip:** put the addresses on mailing labels before you leave, then just stick them on the card)
❑ Small flashlight
❑ Smallest alarm clock you can find. You don't want to miss a tee time.
❑ Glasses/ contacts/ solutions/ eye glass cleaner cloth
❑ Prescription medicines/Aspirin, Advil or Tylenol/ Moleskin/ antibiotic ointment/small first aid kit in your carry on

- ❏ Credit card and ATM card/some cash. Plan on $100/day for miscellaneous expenses
- ❏ Two golf towels and a golf umbrella (make it a good strong one with vents)
- ❏ Power plug adapter
- ❏ Reading mate (light)
- ❏ Passport (with photocopy in suitcase), driver's license, handicap certificate
- ❏ Energy bars (beverage carts or snack bars are not common on courses in Ireland)

Do not bring:

- Bulky camera
- Heavy shoes
- Plaid shirts
- Shorts with cargo pockets (suggest you leave all shorts at home)
- Heavy paper items such as magazines and travel brochures

Handicap Certificate: Unlike some courses in Scotland, a handicap certificate is not required for play on any courses in Ireland. However, according to Brian Keogh, if you are traveling to Ireland during the summer months (warning, the term "summer" may be misleading) many clubs organize an "Open Week." According to him, "It does exactly what it says on the tin—competitions are open to anyone with an official handicap certificate and entry fees are usually modest."

Passport and airline tickets: To avoid delays, make sure you advise the ticketing travel agent of the exact spelling of your name as it appears on your passport. Carry your passport and tickets with you and secure them on arrival at your hotel.

Leisure clothing: Put together one good-quality quick drying outfit and wear it for sightseeing.

Formal clothing: In general, you will not need formal clothing on your golf tour to Ireland. However, if your tour includes lunch or dinner at a deluxe hotel for example, there may be a dress code; if applicable to your itinerary, you should pack a jacket, dress shirt and tie. Before you finalize your packing list, contact the golf club(s) and check on dress requirements.

Smoking: More frequent in Europe, although most restaurants now have non-smoking sections and all pubs in Ireland are now non-smoking. Pipe and cigarette smoking are generally more tolerated in Ireland than cigars. Private clubs may have private rooms where smoking is permitted.

XI.

TRAVELING WITHIN IRELAND

*"The gladdest moment in human life, methinks, is a
departure into unknown lands. The blood flows with
the fast circulation of childhood."*
Sir Richard Burton (1821-1890)

INFORMATION IN THIS section will advise you
on what services you can expect to find in Ireland and
important information that will allow you to travel safely
and comfortably throughout the island.

Laundry

Dry cleaning, laundry and pressing services in European
hotels can be very expensive. Fortunately, you won't need
this service on a golf trip unless your stay is longer than
usual or extended beyond your original plan by unforeseen
events.

Long-Distance Telephone Calls

Long-distance telephone calls placed from hotel guest
rooms are subject to high service charges. When making a

call, place it collect or use a long distance calling card with a local access number. Cell phones can be used, but calls are pricey; check with your carrier to find out the details for your plan.

Sugar and Salt Substitutes

Visitors whose diets call for these substitutes should bring ample quantities of your favorite because they are not commonly found in Irish restaurants.

Time and Time Difference

Ireland is on Greenwich Mean Time (or GMT) which is five hours ahead of US Eastern Standard time and one hour behind Continental European time. Similar to Daylight Savings in the U.S., clocks in Ireland are put forward one hour at the end of March and back one hour at the end of October. During the longest days of summer, it stays light until as late as 2300 hrs (11 pm). In mid-December it can be dark by 1600 hrs (4 pm).

Electric Current

The standard electricity supply is 220 volts AC in the Republic of Ireland and 240 volts AC in Northern Ireland (50 cycles). Visitors need a plug adaptor (to enable standard American 2-pin plugs to work in standard Irish or UK 3-pin plugs), which can be bought at airports, discount stores, or electrical suppliers. When using 110-volt appliances, such as an electric razor or hair dryer, you also need to attach a current converter appropriate for the wattage of the appliance. You will want to use this system to recharge your phone, email device, and digital camera. *TIP: If you can, leave unnecessary electrical gadgets including hair dryers at home. Many guesthouses, B&B's and most hotels provide hair dryers.*

Visit **www.kropla.com/electric.htm** a world electric guide, for information on important issues on using electronic devices (including laptop computers) in other countries.

Passports and valuables

Make several photocopies of your passport. Leave one at home and carry an extra in your luggage in case your passport is lost or stolen. Safeguard any valuables (leave expensive jewelry at home) and passport in your hotel's safe-deposit box on arrival.

Jetlag

There are dozens of theories on avoiding jetlag and countless articles describing them. Extensive medical research has also been done on the subject. Use the word *jetlag* to search the Internet for detailed information. Try **www.bodyclock.com**. It does help if you can stay awake on arrival (after overnight travel) and move as quickly as possible into the rhythm of the country to which you have traveled. As we mentioned earlier, a relaxing fun round of golf upon arrival will tire you out nicely and get you ready for bed on the local schedule.

Smart International Travel Tips

For excellent advice on how to travel safely and comfortably visit **www.europetravelhub.com/traveling-europe/travel-tips**.

Main Street in Killarney showing the Flesk Restaurant at the junction of Plunkett and Main Streets. If you look really hard, you can see a sign pointing the way to a golf course. Thus, this photo reinforces the need to have one person drive and another act as navigator!

Photo Credit: Bill Ruskin

Passport/Visa Requirements

A valid US passport is required to visit the island of Ireland. Visitors of all other nationalities should contact their local Irish Embassy/Consulate prior to traveling to the

Republic of Ireland and visitors to Northern Ireland should contact their local British Embassy, High Commission, or Consular Office. Embassy and Consulate contact details are listed below.

Embassy of Ireland, 2234 Massachusetts Ave., N.W., Washington D.C. 20008.
Tel: (202) 462-3939

UK Embassy, 3100 Massachusetts Ave., N.W., Washington D.C. 20008
Tel: (202) 588-7800

Consulate of Ireland, 345 Park Ave., 17th Floor, New York, NY 10154.
Tel: (212) 319-2555

Consulate of UK, 845 Third Ave., New York, NY 10022.
Tel: (212) 745-0200

The Embassy of the United States of America, Dublin, 42 Elgin Road, Dublin 4.
Tel: +353 (0) 1 6687122

The US Consulate General, 14 Queen Street, Belfast BT1 6EQ.
Tel: +44 (0) 28 9032 8239

Republic of Ireland
For further information, contact the Department of Foreign Affairs,
Tel: +353 (0) 1 478 0822.

For a list of Irish Embassies, visit **www.irlgov.ie/ iveagh**

Northern Ireland
Further information is available from your local UK Embassy or Consulate. For other details, contact the Foreign and Commonwealth Office at **www. fco.gov.uk**

Medical

Private medical insurance is highly recommended for visitors from the United States. Please check with your carrier regarding your coverage before departure.

> *Republic of Ireland Department of Agriculture and Food*:
> Tel: +353 (0) 1 607 2000 or visit **www.irlgov.ie** or *Department of Health and Children* Tel: +353 (0) 1 635 4000 or visit **www.doh.ie**

> *Northern Ireland Department of Health, Social Services and Public Safety*
> Tel: +44 (0) 28 9052 0500 or visit **www.dhsspsni. gov.uk**

Visitors with Disabilities

Ireland extends a warm welcome to visitors with disabilities. Many public places and visitor attractions are accessible to wheelchair users, and an increasing number of hotels and restaurants are well equipped to accommodate guests who have any kind of disability. Useful contacts include:

> *Republic of Ireland National Disability Authority,*
> Tel: +353 (0) 1608 0400 or visit **www.nda.ie**

> *Northern Ireland Disability Authority*
> Tel:+44(0)2890297880orvisit**www.disabilityaction. org**

Senior Citizens

Men and women of age 65 and over are recognized as Senior Citizens or (somewhat less elegantly!) Old Age Pensioners and enjoy a variety of discounts and privileges.

Students

Ireland is student friendly, with many attractions offering a reduced student rate or admission charge on presentation of a valid ID card.

Pets

We doubt that anyone would want to bring pets along on a golf tour, but, just in case you are so inclined, we more than highly recommend that you leave them at home because any pets entering the island of Ireland from the US are subject to six months quarantine unless they have undergone the requirements of the UK Pet Travel Scheme and obtained the requisite "Passport for Pets" and entered Ireland through the UK. For more information relating to pets contact:

Republic of Ireland Department of Agriculture Tel: +353 (0) 1 607 2000 or visit **www.irlgov.ie**

Northern Ireland Department of Agriculture and Rural Development
Tel: +44 (0) 28 905 24715 or visit **www.dardni. gov.uk**

Public Holidays

Republic of Ireland
New Years Day	1st January
St. Patrick's Day	17th March
Easter Monday	varies
May Bank Holiday	1st May
June Bank Holiday	5th June
August Bank Holiday	7th August
October Bank Holiday	30th October
Christmas Day	25th December
St. Stephen's Day	26th December

Northern Ireland
New Years Day	1st January
St. Patrick's Day	17th March
Good Friday	varies
Easter Monday	varies
May Bank Holiday	1st May
May Bank Holiday	29th May
July Bank Holiday	12th July
August Bank Holiday	28th August
Christmas Day	25th December
Boxing Day	26th December

Background Notes

For country descriptions, travel warnings, entry requirements, medical facilities, crime information, drug penalties, terrorist threats, safety, Embassy/Consulate location and other information on Ireland, visit the US Department of State at **www.state.gov.com**. Go to *Countries and Regions*, and *Background Notes*. This is an excellent site to bookmark and check when planning travel to any foreign country.

Currency

Here are some important *TIPS* to assist golfers in handling foreign transactions:

- The euro is the currency of the Republic of Ireland. One euro consists of 100 cents. Notes are €5, €10, €20, €50, €100, €200, and €500. Coins are 1c, 2c, 5c, 10c, 20c, 50c, €1, €2.
  Find out more about the euro at **www.europa.eu**
- The monetary unit in Northern Ireland is the British Pound Sterling (£). There are different types of British Pound notes: *English, Scottish, Northern Ireland, and Channel Islands.* They are all equivalent in value and interchangeable. There are 100 pence to each pound. Notes are £5, £10, £20, £50 and £100. Coins are 1p, 2p, 5p, 10p, 20p, 50p, £1 and £2.
- The exchange rate between the US dollar and the Euro and British Pound Sterling fluctuates day to

day. When making purchases with a credit card, the rate of exchange may vary from the time of purchase to the time the charge is actually processed by the credit card issuer. Check the financial section of your local newspaper, *The Wall Street Journal*, or *USA Today* for current exchange rates. Better yet, visit **www.xe.com** for the universal currency converter. This site is the most popular currency tool on the Internet, allowing you to perform interactive foreign exchange rate calculations using live, up to the minute exchange rates for all currencies.

- It is not easy to exchange euro or Scottish, Northern Ireland and Channel Island notes when you return to the USA. Leave your euro and UK coins behind. Buy something or give them to a charity. American banks certainly do not want your foreign coins. Golfers will come out ahead if dollars are brought back when leaving Ireland rather than exchanging through their bank at home. Some (but not very many) airport currency exchanges offer the opportunity to exchange any unused euros or British notes into dollars without charge as you leave the country. (Others charge a pretty penny for this service, too). Check with an airport currency exchange site on arrival in Ireland and plan ahead for your departure accordingly.

- If a receipt is issued when purchasing foreign currency, keep it. Depending on the exchange agent, it may be necessary to turn in a receipt before being allowed to buy US currency.

- John Hagen, world traveler and author of 'Play Away Please', offers the following suggestions on currency exchange and his preferences on money matters:

"I do not take travelers checks, at all, any more. The conversion rates fluctuate too much. If you have a Capital One credit card they are "gold" as they are the only issuer that I know who does not "double-dip" you on the conversion, on use, and then take a fee on top of that as Bank of America, for instance, does, when you make a purchase.

"When you land in Ireland, change at least $300, as the fee is the same as if you only converted $100. If you know where you're staying and what the costs are, approximately, I would change a bunch of USD at the airport and pay the hotels mostly in cash. 5% fees add up. Do not change money at hotels; the fees are a premium. Change at the airport or other location and just bite-the-bullet. AMEX's fees can also run more than others.

"I do use ATMs, yes, but again be prepared for the bank fee, unfortunately.

"I would also call your bank and credit card company and advise them of your travel, as most banks are very watchful these days on unusual transactions. (I call mine, a small bank, and tell them when I'm leaving and when I'm returning.) Two weeks ago, for instance, someone tried to buy a car in Paris with my ATM number. This was weird because I was in the UK and had the card in my possession. The same day, the card number was also used in London to buy tires. My bank caught both frauds. Identity theft is, unfortunately, a part of life these days. This sort of thing has not happened to me for some years, however.

"I also register with the Department of State when I travel and recommend you do the same. This is the website: **www.travel.state.gov**. Surprisingly, if there is a disturbance, they do contact you to advise you about it."

Credit and Debit Cards

All major credit and debit cards are generally accepted on the island of Ireland.

- Exchange rates vary from place to place, but generally the best rate is found in ATMs. A service fee is usually added.
- Any credit card that bears the Visa, MasterCard, or American Express emblem will be widely accepted in Ireland. Visitors with other cards should ask in advance or note whether the card is on display where they wish to use it.

In summary, all you need (money wise) for your golfing tour in Ireland is a credit card and a few euros (or pounds if you are in Northern Ireland) in your pocket each day. ATMs are readily available to access local currency.

TIP: Use ATMs frequently, taking only the cash you need for a day or two to get the best exchange rates and avoid ending up with a lot of Euros or pounds when it's time to depart for the USA.

VAT

Purchases made in Ireland are subject to the VAT (Value Added Tax) of approximately 21.5 %, which is included in the purchase price of the goods and services. Fortunately, you are eligible to recover the VAT in most cases for items you're taking or sending home. If you don't buy very much, it is probably not worth the time or trouble to seek a refund.

But, you will want to follow this procedure to get a refund for more expensive purchases:

1. You must be a non-European Union visitor to Ireland to be able to claim a tax refund. Look for the "tax free shopping" sign in the windows of participating stores.

2. When purchasing items, secure an official VAT receipt and an envelope addressed to the store (refunds are voluntary, so check with the store to see if they will cooperate before you buy). Some stores have a VAT desk or department, at which you need to produce your passport, so be sure it isn't back at your hotel.

3. When leaving Ireland, present the form to the customs official for stamping and have the goods in your carry-on luggage for inspection. Take the form to the airport's *bank window* where you should get your refund.

4. If step three doesn't work, another method is to mail the form back to the store before you leave the country, retaining your receipt. Eventually you will receive a check in American dollars or a credit on your credit card, which is the best way to buy in the first place.

5. VAT is charged on almost everything, but remember that refunds only apply to goods being taken out of the country, not services.

6. You can avoid all of the above by asking the store to ship the goods back to the States for you. This way you avoid the VAT but will of course have to pay for the shipping. For detailed information on this subject visit **www.eurunion.org/legislat/vatweb.htm**.

Tipping

Tipping in Ireland is up to the discretion of the guest but welcomed by the staff and individuals providing the services. Here are some general guidelines. Other services such as laundry and hairdressers often have the gratuity built into the cost of the service. Ask if you are not sure if the gratuity is included.

Category	*Suggested Tip*
Caddie	€12 or £10 per caddie per round
Taxi Driver	10% of fare
Housekeeper	€2.50-3.50 or £2-3
Wait Staff	10-15% of bill, if not included
Tour Drivers	€6-12 or £5-10 (group tip per person at end of tour)
Porters	€1 or £1 per bag

In Pubs: tipping bar staff is not expected and at the customer's discretion. (We recommend you leave a tip unless the service is atrocious; it's really the decent thing to do.)

In Guest Houses and B&B's: Before checking out, it's a nice gesture to leave 5-10 € on the dresser. Although not expected, the staff will be very appreciative.

Personal Expenses

You will incur personal expenses on your trip. Some of them may include: gasoline, mini-bar in room, tipping, phone calls, bar bills, all meals not specified, laundry, souvenirs and gifts. *TIP:* plan on $100 per day for miscellaneous out-of-pocket expenses.

Calling Ireland from the USA

Dial 011 (international long distance) 353 (country code for Ireland) then the number in Ireland dropping the first (0) in the number Example: to call for tourist information in Dublin dial: 011 353 160 57700. Many offices have 800 numbers so you can call toll free from the US (See appendix).

Calling within Ireland

Drop the 011-353; use the '0' and the remainder of the number. Example: to call for tourist information while in Dublin, dial: 0 160 57700.

Directory enquiries Tel: 11811 or visit **www. goldenpages.ie**

Northern Ireland

When calling Northern Ireland from the USA dial 011, 44 (country code for Northern Ireland), then the number, dropping the first '0' in the number. Example: To call the Belfast Tourist Welcome Center dial
011 44 28 9024 6609.

Calling within Northern Ireland

To call within Northern Ireland, drop the 011 44, use the '0' and the rest of the number: 0 28 9024 6609.

Mobile Phones

Only digital phones with GSM subscriptions and a roaming agreement will work on the island of Ireland. Visitors should consult with their providers before leaving.

Pay Phones

Easy-to-use country calling cards are widely available at many outlets.

Mail

Office Opening Hours

Post offices are generally open from 0900-1730 or 9 am-5:30 pm, Monday through Friday in the Republic of Ireland and Northern Ireland. Main post offices also open on Saturdays from 0900-1230 or 9 am-12:30 pm in Northern Ireland and 0900-1700 or 9 am-5 pm in the Republic of Ireland. Please note that exact opening hours vary depending on the size and location of the branch.

Mail Charges

The cost of mailing a standard letter or postcard is:

	Republic of Ireland	Northern Ireland
Within Ireland	€ 0.55	£ 0.41
To Britain	€ 0.82	£ 0.41
To the US	€ 0.82	£ 0.67
To Europe	€ 0.82	£ 0.60

E-mail

Internet cafes can be found in large towns and cities throughout the island of Ireland. Many libraries also have Internet facilities. Your hotel may also offer Internet services, but most likely for a fee.

Personal Safety

Though the general level of personal safety is high, should you be unfortunate enough to fall victim to a crime contact:

Republic of Ireland
Tourist Victim Support, Block 1, Garda HQ, Harcourt Square, Dublin Tel: +353 (0)1 478 5295. Email: **info@ touristvictimsupport.ie** or visit **www.touristvictimsupport. ie.**

Northern Ireland
Contact the local Police station where support will be available. Tel: +44 (0) 28 9065 0222 or visit **www.psni. police.uk** or Email: **info@psni.pnn.police.uk.**

Emergency Numbers

Republic of Ireland
Emergency Services (Police, Fire, Ambulance) Tel: 112 or 999

Northern Ireland
Emergency Services (Police, Fire, Ambulance) Tel: 999

Pubs, Restaurants and Hotels

Drinking Age

The legal drinking age is 18. Some pubs will insist on patrons being over 21 and carrying some form of identification. (Legislation in the Republic of Ireland stipulates that children under 18 are not allowed in premises that serve alcohol after 2130 hrs or 9:30 pm).

Pub Operating Hours

Keep in mind that pub operating hours vary in Ireland, depending on where the house is located. Religious laws used to dictate pub open and closing times i.e., 2:00 pm-11:00 pm but all of that has changed since the mid 1990's.

Pubs in the Republic of Ireland are open seven days a week, usually from 1030 hours (10:30 am). Closing times vary through the week but usually range from 2330 hours (11:30 pm) Monday-Thursday and from 0030 hours (12:30 am) Friday-Saturday. Sunday opening hours are from 1230-2300 hours (12:30 pm-11 pm).

Generally, opening hours in Northern Ireland are 1130-2300 hours (11:30 am-11 pm) Monday-Saturday and 1230-2200 hours (12:30 pm-10 pm) Sunday. Many pubs have extended opening hours, particularly on the weekend.

Some pubs have a "lock-in" where the door is closed to new patrons but those inside are invited to remain until the pub closes. Consider yourself fortunate if you find yourself in a "lock-in" as a part of your Irish Experience. If you buy a couple of rounds and the bartender determines you are not shy with your hard earned cash, you might be invited to hang around after the normal closing time.

So what happens in the pubs after the lock-in? Basically it is the little known realm of stories and experiences that people have garnered over the years. Most of the time, the host or barman does the talking to "captive" ears but occasionally the floor is opened to all comers and stories may be swapped with other nocturnal guests such as police, politicians, doctors and a broad spectrum of night fliers who may happen to be there at closing time. Heady times for those fortunate to be *"locked-in."*

Smoking Restrictions

Smoking is not allowed in public areas, such as pubs, restaurants, hotels, or public vehicles in the Republic of Ireland. Northern Ireland also enforces this same smoking ban in public areas, but they go on to include phone booths and enclosed bus/train shelters.

Store Opening Hours

Stores are generally open Monday through Saturday 0900 to 1800 hrs (9 am to 6 pm) with late night shopping until 2000 or 2100 hrs (8 or 9 pm) on Thursdays in many large stores. Sunday opening hours are generally mid day until 1700 or 1800 hrs (5 or 6 pm) or, in Northern Ireland 1300 to 1700 hrs (1 pm to 5 pm)).

Customs

Customs operates green and red channels at most ports and airports. If you need to declare goods in excess of the duty and tax-free allowances for non-EU visitors, you must use the red channel. Pass through the green channel if you have nothing to declare.

Weights and Measurements

The Metric System has been adopted in the Republic of Ireland and Northern Ireland but is not always evident. For example, distance is measured in both miles and kilometers; drinks in pubs come in pints and gasoline comes in liters; while food is sold in both pounds and kilograms.

1 kilometer	= 0.621 miles (multiplying by 0.6 is close enough)
1 mile	= 1.609 km (multiplying by 1.6 is close enough)
1 kilogram	= 2.205 lbs. (multiplying by 2.2 is close enough)
1 lb.	= 0.454 kgs. (multiplying by 0.5 is close enough)
1 liter	= 0.22 UK gallon
1 UK gallon	= 4.546 liters
1 liter	= 0.26 US gallon
1 liter	= 1.06 US quart
1 UK gallon	= 1.25 US gallon

Remember: Go prepared—plan well ahead!

XII.

GETTING AROUND IN IRELAND

"I returned to Ireland. Ireland green and chaste and foolish. And when I wandered over my own hills and talked again to my own people I looked into the heart of this life and saw that it was good."
Patrick Kavanagh, The Green Fool

Rental Cars (Hire Cars)

A hire car is essential for a successful golf tour in Ireland, unless you join a tour group that travels by bus or hire a guide and driver for your tour. Your travel agent can arrange for a hire car or if you prefer, you can do it yourself or let your tour company make arrangements. If you hire a vehicle, your satisfaction is very dependent on how well you handle the driving. So, the more you know about hiring and driving a car in Ireland the better off you will be on your tour. EuropeCar, a leading auto rental company, offers an excellent on line "Guide to Irish Driving" including *Road Signs, Roundabouts, Safety Tips, Driving a Van* and links to other helpful information at **www.europcar.ie/driving. htm**

If you are going to drive in Ireland, it is recommended that you purchase a copy of the *Highway Code of Northern Ireland and Great Britain* SBN 0115522905-5, and read up on the driving rules. The Republic of Ireland has a similar publication on highway codes. You can also go to the website for **353 Car Rental** (see below), which covers all driving laws, conditions, and charges relating to car rentals in Ireland. It also covers the use of credit cards, license requirements, pickup and delivery conditions, fuel, age limits, accidents, towing and traffic.

Car Rental Companies

Cars from the following major hire firms can be reserved for pick up at all major arrival locations including airports at Dublin, Shannon, Kerry, Galway, and Cork, as well as other locations throughout Ireland.

Thrifty: www.thrifty.ie

Europcar: www.europcar.com

Avis: www.myguideireland.com/avis

Hertz: www.hertz.com

Enterprise Rent-a-Car: www.enterprise.com

353 Car Rental: www.353carrental.ie/

Driving

A valid U.S. driver's license is sufficient to drive in Ireland; drivers are obliged by law to carry their license at all times. Seatbelts must be worn at all times, in both the front and the back seats of the vehicle. Motorcyclists and their passengers must wear helmets.

Just as in the UK, traffic in Ireland moves on the left side of the road. Although this convention is initially intimidating for most Americans, they usually adapt fairly quickly. For one thing, the cost of making a mistake is enough to create the needed additional vigilance. As mentioned later in this chapter in the guide to driving on the left side, it really helps to have a front seat passenger serving as a copilot and navigator.

Ireland has very strict laws on drinking and driving, and they are scrupulously enforced. Perhaps the best advice is simply *don't drink and drive*. If you do want to drink, you'll need to designate a non-drinking driver, just as the native Irish do when celebrating.

Another potentially confusing point for Americans is that speed limits in the Republic of Ireland are expressed in kilometers per hour (km/h) because of the country's entry into the European Union. In the Republic, the speed limit is 120 km/h or 75 mph on motorways, 100 km/h or 62 mph on national routes, 80 km/h or 50 mph on local and regional roads and 50 km/h or 31 mph in built-up areas.

Because Northern Ireland is a different country, motorists need to understand that some driving laws are different from the Republic Ireland, including the speed limits. In Northern Ireland, the speed limit is 50 km/h or 31 mph in built-up areas, 100 km/h or 62 mph on the open road and 110 km/h or 70 mph on motorways, unless shown otherwise.

Typical Car Rental Terms and Condition

Each of the various rental car companies has a website (listed earlier) that provides valuable information on driving in Ireland. It also explains its specific *terms and conditions of the rental agreement.* We suggest that you understand your agreement before arriving in Ireland. These terms can include Collision Damage Reduction Insurance (CDR) and Damage Excess Reduction Insurance (DEI).

Rental Vehicle Descriptions

Although 4-door sedans with standard and automatic shift are available for hire and suitable for two travelers, we strongly recommend that groups of four secure a vehicle called a *people carrier* (analogous to a minivan) with adequate space in back for four sets of luggage and four golf bags. A *Sharan, Citroen C8* and *Peugeot* fit this category but have limited luggage space. However, seats can be removed (except on one-way rentals) to gain additional space for luggage.

Among the carrier models that are the most popular with American golfers is the *Volkswagen Caravelle* or *Transporter* designed as a nine-seat people carrier plus luggage and is available in automatic or manual transmission. This vehicle is very comfortable, can be reserved with an automatic transmission (plan ahead), and is ideally suited for six golfers with adequate space for luggage and golf clubs. You need to plan ahead since there is limited availability in

July and August for the people carriers, especially the VW Caravelle.

TIP: Rent an Automatic Shift

While a standard shift car is cheaper to hire, and more readily available than an automatic shift, we recommend that you request an automatic shift.

The automatic is useful because there are enough things to get used to when you sit on the right hand side of the vehicle and drive on the left side of the road. Having an automatic means you don't have to learn how to shift with your left hand, which can be one of the greatest challenges you'll face during your tour, next to getting out of a pot bunker. *More tips on driving on the left-hand side of the road are coming up.*

Platinum and Gold Credit Cards

Whenever possible, use a Platinum or Gold credit card to rent the vehicle so that you can decline the Collision Damage Waiver (CDW) Insurance Option and cut down on your weekly rental rate. Other insurance is mandatory and included in the rental quotation. Some companies offer different escalating insurance coverages with different costs and your credit card coverage may replace them. Some rental agreements are fully comprehensive and everything is included in the price. In this case, there are no hidden costs or extras, other than the excess if you have a bump or someone bumps you. Of course, it is your responsibility to know exactly the *Terms and Conditions* of your contract before driving off the lot.

You now have enough information to know you have to protect your own best interest when working with your chosen rental car company. Be sure to check with your auto insurance company and carefully read the detailed "guide to benefits" pamphlet of the credit card you intend to use well in advance, so that there are no surprises.

It is also a good idea to consult with your American insurance company to find out what advice they can offer for driving overseas.

Success With A Rental Car Means A Successful Trip

The rental and use of a vehicle in Ireland is a very integral part of a successful golf tour. To recap, here are some very important *TIPS*:

- Your car will be a right hand drive. Get acquainted with left hand shift and instruments before leaving the pick-up point. If not offered, ask the hire company for a full demonstration of the controls.
- You drive on the left side of the road.
- Check with your insurance company and credit card carrier before leaving for coverage in the event of an accident.
- Use seat belts. **It's the law.**
- You must be over 21 to rent a car.
- OBEY Speed Limits!
- There is no minimum speed unless posted but it is against the law to do less than 30 miles per hour on a Motorway Highway (like the interstate in the USA).
- Roads are safe but narrow. Avoid night driving if possible.

- Request and pay extra for an automatic shift (about 35% more) but worth it.
- In May 2011, the cost of gasoline (called "petrol") was about €1.50 per liter in the Republic and £1.30 per liter in Northern Ireland. With the world oil supply in turmoil, be prepared for fluctuating petrol prices. Visit **www.theaa.com/motoring** for a current fuel price report in all European countries. Check this website, which is managed by the UK/Irish equivalent of the AAA in the U.S., for current fuel costs before traveling.
- A so-called "full size" car in Europe is about the size of a compact in America. We recommend renting a "people carrier" for each party of four golfers.
- On roundabouts (traffic circles) give way to traffic *on your right.*
- Avoid driving in bus or bicycle lanes, which is a road traffic offense!
- Pass only on the outside (right) lane (don't even attempt to pass until you are very confident with left lane driving).
- In general, roads in the Ireland are narrower and have more curves than in America. Allow plenty of time between destinations and drive safely. Visit **www.iol.ie/~discover/driving.htm**, print off the driving signs and become familiar with them before departing for Ireland.

Driving on the Left Hand Side

Advice from the founder of Master Drive, a professional driving school for teenagers in Colorado:

A few years ago, my wife and I had a great trip to Europe. We spent a lot of time driving in England, mostly in the Cotswold area, as well as in Scotland. We certainly enjoyed the countryside, but since they drive on the "wrong" side of the road and sit on the "wrong" side of the car, it became a challenge for a while. Especially when you come to a "roundabout," or a "double roundabout," and you are very busy just trying to avoid being hit!

In addition to the risk to your body, there is a big factor in regard to liability. When driving in a foreign environment, being unaware of the local laws and rules of the road is not going to help you defend yourself. This is a very serious matter, and you could find yourself in deep trouble if you are careless, so don't take this lightly.

The most important thing to consider is that driving in most other countries, especially on the "wrong side" of the road is *very different*. When driving in the USA, you are doing most things automatically without even thinking about it because you have a *program* in your brain to do most things at the *subconscious* level. But in a totally new environment, you are forced to do more things at the *conscious* level. The more things you have to do at the conscious level, the lower your performance. This is true in anything and everything we do.

The most effective strategy you can use for this challenge is a "driving partnership" with another golfer acting as a partner. When driving in a foreign environment, you are going to need some help from the partner. Sometimes, this may be difficult for men to do because most of them believe that they have received God-created super driving skills as part of their DNA. Maybe, but the DNA seems to work only for driving in the good old USA.

TIP: Add a GPS unit and the driving will be easier and safer. But it's still a good idea to have another person do the navigating to allow the driver to concentrate on the driving.

It's possible to buy a GPS unit for the UK and Ireland from stores in the US or online; if you're really lucky, you may be able to find one on eBay. And, of course, when you're back home and don't need it any more, you can sell it to someone else, or keep it so you can loan it to friends who are going. Or, more importantly, you can hold onto it so you can use it for your next golf trip to Ireland or Scotland!

If you don't buy, you can rent a GPS with highway, street and destination information from **www.gpsrental@lowergear.com**. Enter your travel dates for the selected GPS and an order confirmation is sent to your email address. The GPS is shipped to arrive about two days prior to your departure date to give you time to get familiar with the unit before you leave. You pay rent only on the days on your reservation, plus the to-and-from shipping as charged by UPS. A pre-authorization on your credit card is made before shipping, but the final charges are not made until after the GPS is returned. Once you have received the GPS, experiment and get familiar with it prior to leaving for your trip. The GPS will have an intuitive touch screen with very clear and easy to read menus. Golf courses can be found under "Points of Interest" or you can enter the street addresses for your selected courses. A prepaid return-shipping label will be in the box with the unit delivered to you. Re-box the unit when you get back to the US and drop it off at any authorized UPS shipping facility.

Even with a GPS, the front-seat partner must take on the role of navigator, working in cooperation with the driver. Believe me, four eyes and two brains are necessary for driving safely in a foreign environment. An attitude of cooperation and understanding is critically important!

In order to make this partnership work effectively, it may be good to sit for a while and discuss some of the basic information, instruments, signs, highway numbers, speed limits, directions, specific landmarks, and get familiar with the GPS, etc. The navigator *is* going to make some mistakes so accept this from the start; and for your health's sake, the driver must just follow orders and be totally focused upon the *driving*.

BOTTOM LINE: If you are going to be driving in Ireland or any foreign country, prepare yourself as much as possible. Get information about road signs, their meaning and laws and plan ahead. It really can be a lot of fun if you treat it like a good "road rally" (not to be confused with racing.) Treat it like a game and enjoy the challenge.

And Beeee Smoooooth!

Ronn Langford
Founder, MasterDrive, Inc.
Colorado Springs, CO USA

Bill Ruskin's Experience with Left Hand Driving

Several years ago while driving in Scotland, my wife and I hit a low curb and blew out the left front tire almost immediately after starting our first motor trip of the vacation. The same thing happened during our latest trip to Ireland. We whacked a curb with the front wheel while squeezing to the extreme left to avoid an oncoming vehicle. We had to pay to replace it and it was very expensive. This is the most common accident that happens to drivers unfamiliar with left-hand driving in Ireland and the UK. The roads are narrow, and there are miles of neat, rough edge curb lines just waiting to be struck by a tire (before accepting the vehicle, read the fine print in your contract or ask if your rental agreement covers tire damage, wheels, hubcaps and side mirrors that are commonly torn off in minor collisions). The best way to avoid this type of damage is to focus on the center line and don't try to balance your vehicle between the centerline and the curb. As Ronn says, "the driver really has to focus on the driving." Let someone else do the navigating and trust the GPS system.

Gas (Petrol)

There is a good network of gas or petrol stations throughout Ireland, selling unleaded gas and diesel. For further information, obtain a copy of Tourism Ireland's 'Touring Ireland by Car' brochure. Download the brochure at **www.discoverireland.com/us/ireland-plan-your-visit/downloadablebrochures.**

A reminder that petrol is relatively expensive in Ireland. For motoring advice and current fuel prices on the island and other European countries visit **www.aaireland.ie**.

Inland Ferries & Island Boat Services

When visiting any of the offshore islands dotting the Irish coastline, check out island boat services well in advance—and check again just before traveling since changes in the weather may affect services. Regular island boat services operate to the Aran Islands off the Galway coast, Rathlin Island off the North Antrim coast, Aranmore Island off Donegal, Clare Island off the Mayo coast, Sherkin and Cape Clear Island off the coast of west Cork. There are also several inland ferry services that ease traveling around Ireland and make the journey more interesting, such as the Strangford Lough ferry at Portaferry, County Clare, and the ferry link between Greencastle, County Donegal, and Magilligan Point, County Londonderry.

Public Transport

Public transportation systems are superior in Ireland and one can get anywhere by bus, train or taxi. However, it is not practical to plan a golf tour to Ireland using public transportation.

Irish Rail—Larnród Éireann
Tel: +353 (0) 1 836 6222 or visit **www.irishrail.ie**

Irish Bus—Bus Éireann
Tel: +353 (0) 1 836 6111 or visit **www.buseireann.ie**

Irish Bus—Bus Átha Cliath
Tel: +353 (0) 1 873 4222 or visit **www.dublinbus.ie**

Republic of Ireland
The Dublin area is served by the 'Dart'—Rapid Transit Rail—from Howth to Malahide in North County Dublin via Dun Laoghaire to Greystones in County Wicklow. The new Dublin Luas tram system is a state of the art Light Rail Transit (LRT) network connecting outlying suburbs to Dublin city center with a high capacity, high frequency,

high speed service. When in the Republic of Ireland call Luas at 1800 300 604 or visit **www.luas.ie**.

Northern Ireland

Translink (Northern Ireland Railways, Ulsterbus, Belfast City bus) Tel: +44 (0) 28 9066 6630 or **www. translink.co.uk**. Check for specially discounted fares when traveling by public transport. For instance, the Freedom of Northern Ireland/Emerald Card/Irish Rover tickets offer unlimited bus/train travel for 3,5,8, or 15 days.

Taxis

Metered taxis are available in Belfast, Dublin, Galway, Limerick and Cork. In other areas, fares should be agreed upon beforehand. In Belfast and Londonderry, share-taxi services operate like mini-buses. Taxis are usually found at ranks in central locations and do not usually cruise the streets. Be aware of your surroundings and know about how far and how long it takes to get to your destination; you don't want to be driven in circles or taken the long way. Unfortunately, some cab drivers will take you on a ride to run up the meter. Take proper precautions to make sure this doesn't happen.

Toll Charges

There are very few toll roads in Ireland. There are toll charges (€1.80) for using the new M50 (Dublin Orbital Motorway) and M1 Northern Motorway.

Tolls for Tunnels and Bridges
• East Link Bridge (Dublin)

- West Link Bridge (Dublin)
- West Link Bridge 2 (Dublin)

Motorway Tolls
- M1 Toll (Drogheda By-pass)

Regional Airports

The following internal flights operate within Ireland:

Depart	Arrive	Via Airline
Belfast City	Cork	Aer Arann
Dublin	City of Derry	Logan Air
Dublin	Cork	Aer Arann, Ryanair
Dublin	Donegal	Aer Arann
Dublin	Kerry	Aer Arann
Dublin	Galway	Aer Arann
Dublin	Shannon	Aer Lingus
Dublin	Sligo	Aer Arann
Dublin	Knock	Logan Air

Regional Airline Information:

Airline	Telephone	Website
Aer Arann	353 (0) 61 704428	www.aerarann.com
Aer Lingus	1 800 IRISH AIR	www.aerlingus.com
British Airways (Operating as Logan Air)	1 800 AIRWAYS	www.ba.com
Ryanair	0905 566 0000	www.ryanair.com

APPENDIX

Health and a long life to you.
Land without rent to you.
A child every year to you.
And if you can't go to heaven,
May you at least die in Ireland.
                                    Irish Blessing

Glossary

HERE ARE SOME phrases, names, places and things that you may want to become familiar with. The more you know about the history and customs associated with Irish life and golf, the greater you'll enjoy your tour.

Baker's List: In Ireland, you're still alive if you are on the Baker's List

Bits and Bobs: An odd assortment of anything.

Bob, a few: Money: a few pounds or Euros.

Bogway or Boreen: Small country road, laneway, barely a path.

Bramley: Apple-brutish cooks agree that the Bramley is the best cooking apple.

Craic—Conversation, fun and laughter

Deoch don bhaile (pronounced juck dun bowhair)—one for the road, often used to describe the last drink of the night.

Diddle: Make traditional 'mouth music.'

Dia dhuit (dh sounds like a 'g')—Hello

Dosh: Money

Drisheen: Blood Sausage similar to black pudding

Dub: A native of Dublin.

English Justice: Oxymoron: you're presumed innocent until proven Irish.

Failte: Welcome

Fleadh: Fairs, Festivals

Ghillie: A fishing guide

Gouff: The spelling of the game of golf between the 15th and 18th centuries.

Go raibh maith agat (sounds like 'go rev mah agut): Thank you!

Gob: Mouth

Hole in the Wall: Term often used to refer to the ATM machine

Irish Lie: A person walking along a road may ask a farmer the distance to Waterford. If it's six miles the response may be "its only three miles" because the person is walking. Hopefully there are no victims to an Irish Lie.

Lock-in: Heady times for those fortunate to be "locked-in" an Irish pub.

Loops: A term used by club caddies referring to number of times they worked in a given day. For example, "I did two loops today."

Looper: A caddie

Mucker: Mate, Friend

Oiche Mhaith (sounds like eeha wah)—Good Night

Slan (sounds like 'slawn')—Goodbye

Slainte: (*sounds like slawn te*): cheers, good health (useful for the pub after golf)

Traditional Irish food: Irish stew, bacon & cabbage, Irish soda bread

Whacker: Half glass of whiskey

Links Courses: Found around the coast of the British Isles and Ireland, these natural courses follow the untouched contours of the land. They are sandy, and the fine grasses produce tight lies and the ultimate challenge in golf. All the Open Championships are played over links courses. Golfers will be familiar with Carnoustie, St Andrews, Troon, Turnberry, Royal Lytham and St. Annes, and Sandwich.

Parkland Courses: Inland golf courses that have distinctive vegetation, on originally forested land that has deteriorated. Many of these courses are to be found at 500 feet elevation or higher. They have tough grasses, heather, gorse and occasional trees.

Pot Bunkers: Best avoided altogether and difficult to play out of with control. These small but deep sand traps are to be found in strategic spots on all good links courses.

In Town—Going to Dublin City

Using the Internet

As you've learned, this book provides basic information you need to know as you plan your golf adventure in Ireland. For detailed and especially *current* information, it's best to go to the Internet for all aspects of trip planning, including travel, accommodations, currency, safety and weather. Much of the travel-related data becomes outdated soon after a guidebook is published. To help you overcome this limitation, we have developed an extensive listing of categorized websites within this Appendix, such that you should be able to find a place to go for practically everything you'll need or want to know. Of course, our book will give you insights into Ireland, Irish golf, and especially the Irish Experience, but the Internet will certainly be more helpful for discovering updated details about travel and dates of events and festivals in Ireland, as well as helpful images and current fees for the courses you may want to play.

To access recent information about the geographical area you will be visiting, try the websites for local or regional newspapers in your chosen area. To help you get started, this Appendix lists the sites for the major newspapers in Ireland.

The Internet is also a great way to learn more about the country, especially its history, people, customs, festivals and opportunities available to visitors beyond the wonderful golf courses. If you start planning your summer (May-September) golf tour early, you will have the fall and winter months to visit websites to learn all you'd like to know, including details about accommodations and any restaurants or pubs you will be near. Besides, you might find some special Internet-only prices and offers!

In addition to the 75-plus sites listed below, we have also described a dozen interesting and informative books about traveling and playing golf in Ireland.

Maps of Ireland

www.discoverireland.com

Includes an interactive map to plan and explore Ireland. When you get closer to traveling, you can also find a 5-day weather forecast for your specific destinations.

www.tailormadegolftours.com

Also features an interactive golf map of Ireland presented by regions.

www.google.com

Use Google, or your preferred search engine, to look for *map of Ireland* and you will find many different maps of Ireland featuring political boundaries of regions, counties and countries, roadways and other valuable trip planning information.

General Information about Ireland

www.tourismireland.com

A comprehensive helpful website for every aspect of your travel to the island.

www.discoverireland.com

Discover information at this site that will let you custom design a trip to "your very own Ireland." It includes a detailed and up-to-the-minute listing of festivals and events.

www.nitb.com

The official site of the Northern Ireland Tourist Board, it contains unique information about this section of the island.

www.discovernorthernireland.com

Another helpful website for information and contacts in Northern Ireland.

www.irelandseye.com

Provides a wide selection of articles, travel information, and descriptions of attractions and pubs.

www.irishcentral.com

Still another site that offers travel information and facts about attractions; it also can help you shop for Irish goods, including a St Patrick's Day breakfast basket!

www.heritageireland.ie

Lists things to do and see in Ireland with a focus on the island's history.

www.heritagetowns.com

Describes more history, emphasizing towns that especially reflect the Irish Heritage and history.

www.gardensireland.com

Don't miss this site if you want to plan visits to special beautiful houses, castles and gardens in Ireland.

www.heritageisland.com

Brings together information about many great visitor attractions and Heritage Towns on the island of Ireland.

www.magni.org.uk

Use this site to plan visits to the Museums and Galleries of Northern Ireland.

www.nationaltrust.org.uk

The National Trust is responsible for maintaining a huge number of historical and other significant sites in Ireland while keeping them accessible to the public. Be prepared to be overwhelmed by all that you can experience.

www.nimc.co.uk
Another site about museums you can visit when you're not playing golf. This one is maintained by the Northern Ireland Museums Council.

www.shamrock.org
For information on tour packages to Ireland.

www.ireland_fun_facts.com
This site presents an insider's Internet tour of Ireland; filled with Irish traditions, jokes, quotes, maps, blessings and more.

www.dublinevents.com
A complete online guide for planning your stay in Dublin or finding things to do once you arrive.

www.tourismirelandinfo.com
If you're so inclined to add a little business to your pleasure, this site provides information on industry, marketing and commerce.

www.failteireland.ie
Fáilte Ireland is an nonprofit that promotes Ireland in many different ways; this particular address will take you to its corporate website.

www.xe.com
Use this site for up-to-the-minute currency exchange information and instant calculations.

www.irishwhiskeyevent.com

The official website about Irish whiskey; it has plenty of information for you to drink in . . .

www.islandireland.com

This address leads you to an Internet guide that focuses on Irish art, culture and entertainment.

Travel and Related Websites

www.metcheck.com

This website is reliable for weather information that can help you when traveling in Ireland or elsewhere in Europe.

www.weather.com

This familiar U.S. site also allows you to check current weather conditions in specific locations in Ireland as well as the 10-day forecast to help you anticipate the weather conditions you will encounter. This may help you know how to pack.

www.britishairways.com/travel/travelsmart

Even if you're not traveling with British Airways, the site can help you with its international travel information.

www.travel.state.gov

U.S. State Department website is invaluable for information on many aspects of any country you'd like to visit; somewhat drearily, it is the place to go for the latest disease warnings, terrorism alerts and travel restrictions in all countries.

www.cdc.gov

Published by the Centers for Disease Control, this site also has information on diseases and/or health concerns in your destination area.

www.who.int/en

In case you haven't gotten enough warning, the World Health Organization also issues health warnings and alerts to travelers for all countries in the world.

www.tsa.gov/travelers/airtravel/assistant/index.shtm

This site is maintained by the ubiquitous Transportation Security Administration (TSA) in order to provide travelers with current security and travel information.

www.tripadvisor.com

This powerful site offers the best travel information and provides unbiased reviews on thousands of destinations.

www.europa.eu

Go to this site if you want to know more about the euro, the currency of the Republic of Ireland and most other European countries.

www.wsj.com/travel

Visit this site for information on how to land "The best deals on airline tickets" and "The 10 rules of the road for air travel." It will also link you to current travel podcasts with Scott McCartney.

www.dontforgetyourtoothbrush.com

Whether you tend to plan ahead or wait until the last minute, you can use this site's handy, before-you-leave checklists of what to take along.

www.thebathroomdiaries.com

There isn't much to say about this site other than reporting that it contains reviews of 12,000 public bathrooms in 120 countries. We'll bet you didn't know about it.

www.timeanddate.com

This site includes a world clock, a time-zone converter and a calculator that instantly show you the time difference between any two cities anywhere in the world. It's especially helpful for phone calls.

Best Websites for Finding Flight Deals (Other than the Airline sites)

www.expedia.com

www.orbitz.com

www.travelocity.com

www.priceline.com

www.cheaptickets.com

www.lowfares.com

Use these sites to compare fare data on different airlines.

www.kayak.com

www.mobissimo.com

www.sidestep.com

www.farecompare.com

More Sites—Flight Information

www.yapta.com

This amazing personal travel assistant tracks price changes and sends alerts if the price of your exact itinerary has dropped. It may even help you get a refund or voucher for future travel.

www.asaca.com

This one is presented by the United States Air Consolidators Association; consolidators are basically speculators who buy blocks of tickets from airlines well in advance at a discount and hope they can find some tourists to buy them later. You can shop here for lowest possible ticket prices but you'll have to put up with the very lowest level of service.

www.seatguru.com

For you long-legged readers, this site describes different seating arrangements on different airlines to help you search for the best seats.

www.expertflyer.com

Search this website for the best upgrade fares. Look into 'premium economy' in between business class and coach, offering extra legroom and better meal service. Not all airlines offer this class, but expect to find it on longer flights.

www.fly.faa.gov

The site operated by the Federal Aviation Administration lets you check the status of any airport in the country for conditions and information.

www.flightstats.com

This handy site lets you know when any scheduled commercial planes take off and land. Your family and friends can track your flight across the ocean, too.

Accommodations in Ireland

www.irelandhotels.com
The Irish Hotels Federation

www.nihf.co.uk
Northern Ireland Hotels Federation

www.cmvhotels.com
Manor House Hotels and Irish Country Hotels

www.irishfarmholidays.com
For information on Farm House stays

www.nifcha.com

For information on Northern Ireland Farm and Country holidays

www.irelandsbluebook.com

Search for really special places in the Blue Book of Country Homes in Ireland

www.hiddenireland.com

The guide to hidden country homes in Ireland if you relish being off the beaten track

www.tourismresources.ie/fh

Describes a great many friendly bed and breakfast homes in Ireland

www.bandbassociation.org/resources.htm

Bed and Breakfast Association of Northern Ireland and Great Britain

www.bedandbreakfast-directory.co.uk

For a complete directory of Bed and Breakfasts in the UK, including Northern Ireland, and the Republic of Ireland

www.bedandbreakfast.com/northern-ireland.html

For detailed lists of Bed and Breakfasts in Northern Ireland

www.ownerdirect.com/accommodation/ireland

Offers holiday lodging directly from owners of homes

Here are other similar sites:

www.accommodation.ie

www.goireland.com

www.travel-ireland.com

www.irelandyes.com

For Irish Holiday Cottages check out:

www.greatrentals.com/Ireland/Ireland.html

www.irishvacationrental.com

www.homeaway.com/Vacation-rentals-villas/Ireland

www.ImagineIreland.com

Also check any of the various travel websites for affordable accommodations.

Driving in Ireland

www.visit-drivingabroad.co.uk
Driving tips and road signs for all countries.

www.asirt.org
The website for the Association for Safe International Road Travel (ASIRT), Safety information, driving tips, and worldwide road conditions.

www.ricksteves.com

According to Rick Steves, driving in Ireland is basically wonderful—once you remember to stay on the left hand side of the road, get used to driving on the right side of the car, and master those roundabouts.

www.goireland.about.com

This site offers the Top 10 driving tips for Ireland.

www.myguideireland.com/driving-in-ireland

Driving tips for American visitors, including traffic, driving rules, seat belts, speed limits, alcohol, roundabouts, and emergencies.

www.thrifty.ie/aboutdrivingireland.php

This site emphasizes the hot topic of safety, including warnings that drunk driving and speeding are not tolerated. It shows that fines for breaking speed limit laws or any other driving violations are common in Ireland just as in the US, but a whole lot bigger.

www.google.com

Use this or another search engine to look for additional sites on driving in Ireland, information on rental car companies, driving tours, insurance and related topics.

www.viamichelin.com

The tire and travel company can provide you with driving directions for 4.4 million miles of road in 42 European countries. This information can help you plan, but you'll still want a GPS unit in your car.

Dining Out in Ireland

www.findarestaurant.ie
Complete dining guide to restaurants in Ireland. You can also find festivals that involve food.

www.softguides.com/ireland/restaurants/index.html
Eating out in Ireland is quite varied in cuisine and standards vary considerably. Because costs and disappointment can be high, it's best to shop around on this site.

www.foodeu.com/northern-ireland
This is considered by many to be the top guide to eating and dining in Northern Ireland

www.tasteofireland.com
This site allows you to search for restaurants in Ireland by name, location, type of food, and price.

www.zagat.com
Use this site by the famous tour guide publisher to search for the best 25 of Ireland's restaurants.

www.fodors.com
Another site run by a well known guidebook publisher. It describes destinations and nearby hotels and restaurants.

www.tripadvisor.com/restaurants
Not only does this site tell you about restaurants, you can actually make dinner reservations online if you'd like.

Golf in Ireland

www.irishgolfguide.net
Information on the best golf courses in Ireland.

www.irishgolf.net
Searchable Irish golf course directory.

www.igtoa.com
The Irish Golf Tour Operators Association describes its services.

www.irishgolfcourses.co.uk
A complete guide to golf in Ireland, detailed information and color photos on *all* golf courses on the island.

www.discoverireland.ie/golf.aspx
The official Ireland Golf Guide 2011 has information on the excellent courses the island has to offer.

www.gui.ie
The Golfing Union of Ireland is the leading teaching facility in Ireland. Search here under tab *golfers–open fixtures* for information on "open weeks" where visitors can see and compete with locals on their golf clubs.

www.golftoday.co.uk
In perhaps a case of "more than I needed to know," this site describes golf courses in England, Scotland, Wales, Northern Ireland, and the Republic of Ireland, as well as the US, continental Europe and the rest of the world.

www.uk-golf.com

Information, bulletin boards, links course directories for all of the UK.

www.uk-golfguide.com
Another UK golf and travel information site.

www.golf-historian.co.uk
Events, books, videos, gallery on golf history in the UK.

www.worldgolf.com
Possibly golf's most read online publication. It puts massive amounts of information on golf throughout the world at your fingertips.

www.lightningsafety.com
What to do when lightning is near; you'll be best off if you consult this site *before* you play because you might not be able to access the site once the storm closes in on you!

www.mygolfsociety.ie
Offers members of golf societies (golf clubs) a free booking service for other facilities where they are welcome.

Transportation and Communication

www.irishrail.ie
The website for Irish Rail, also called "L'arnrod Eireann".

www.eurail.com/eurail-ireland-pass

Short or long term Eurail passes are available so that you can explore the Republic of Ireland by rail without buying a ticket each time.

www.buseireann.ie
The website for the Irish bus service, called "Eireann."

www.luas.ie
Information on the DART Rapid Transit Rail System in the Dublin area.

www.irelandyes.com/transportation.html
Information on ferries to Ireland and within Ireland and Northern Ireland, as well as other information on airlines, trains and buses.

www.irishferries.co.uk
Get useful facts about ferries operating between Ireland and the UK.

National and Local Irish Newspaper Websites

www.independent.ie
The Irish Independent, news from Ireland and around the world.

www.irishtimes.com
Find the latest Irish news online here

www.herald.ie
Ireland's Evening Herald newspaper online.

www.irisoifigiuil.ie
The Irish State Gazette.

www.theirishbulletin.blogspot.com
Official Irish Republic Gazette.

www.belfasttelegraph.co.uk
Provides news about sports and entertainment for Belfast and County Antrim.

www.ulstergazette.co.uk
Website for Ulster, the largest readership in Armagh City.

www.corkindependent.com
Free weekly newspaper for metropolitan Cork.

www.foinse.ie
National Irish-speaking newspaper.

www.emigrant.ie
News dedicated to the Irish outside of Ireland.

www.echo.ie
Dublin News, sports, jobs, etc.

www.advertiser.ie/galway
Galway newspaper website.

Useful Conversions

Men's Suits and Coats

American	34	36	38	40	42	44	46	48
British	34	36	38	40	42	44	46	48
Continental	44	46	48	51	54	56	59	59

Men's Shirts

American	14	14.5	15	15.5	16	16.5	17	17.5	18
British	14	14.5	15	15.5	16	16.5	17	17.5	18
Continental	36	37	38	39	41	42	43	44	45

Men's Shoes

American	7.5	8.5	9.5	10.5	11.5	12.5	13.5
British	7	8	9	10	11	12	13
Continental	40	41	42	43	44	45	46

Women's Dresses, Coats, Skirts, Pants

American	6	8	10	12	14	16	18
British	8	10	12	14	16	18	20
Continental	38	40	42	44	46	48	50

Women's Shoes

American	4	5	6	7	8	9	10
British	2.5	3.5	4.5	5.5	6.5	7.5	8.5
Continental	34	35	36	37	38	39	40

Temperatures

C (Celsius)	0	5	10	15	20	25	30	35
F (Fahrenheit)	32	40	50	60	70	75	85	95

TIP: For easy metric conversions, visit ***www.sciencemadesimple. net*** for online calculations for unit measurements. Choose the units to convert. Or use an Internet site to convert whatever you want to, such as Miles to Kilometers.

ACKNOWLEDGEMENTS

THE AUTHORS WOULD like to extend their appreciation and thanks to the following organization and other people who assisted in preparing this book:

TOURISM IRELAND

The authors acknowledge and thank *Tourism Ireland* for its support and for their permission to use material in this book from Tourism Ireland publications. Tourism Ireland is the agency responsible for marketing the island of Ireland overseas as a vacation site. Tourism Ireland was established under the framework of the Belfast Agreement of Good Friday, April 1998 to increase tourism to the island of Ireland as a whole. If you would like to contact *Tourism Ireland* to order a free vacation planning kit, visit **www. discoverireland.com** or call 1-800-223-6470.

Anthony Byrne, General Manager Tralee Golf Club, West Barrow, Ardfert, County Kerry

Joe Byrne, Executive Vice-President, Tourism Ireland

George Dushan, Retired media-relations senior specialist for Colorado Springs Utilities and current avid Arizona golfer

Sandy Glenn, Freelance copywriter based in Scottsdale, Arizona

Rev. Fr. Enda Glynn, Official historian of Lahinch Golf Club

John P. Hagen, Author, *'Play Away Please' The Tale of the Sale of Golf's Greatest Icon–The Old Course Starter's Box*

Jim Hayes, Former Publisher of FORTUNE Magazine and retired Chairman of Ashworth, Inc.

John Hehir, Director of Sales & Marketing, Dromoland Castle Newmarket-on-Fergus, County Clare

Brian Higgins, Director of Golf, Waterville Golf Links, Waterville, County Kerry, Ireland

Ray Kearney, Marketing Manager, The Lodge at Doonbeg Golf Club, County Clare

Patrick Lennon, Acting Content Team Manager, Tourism Ireland, Coleraine, Northern Ireland

Padraig McGillicuddy, General Manager, Ballygarry House, Hotel and Spa, Tralee, County Kerry

Graeme McDowell, Professional Golfer, U.S. Open Champion 2010, Portrush, Northern Ireland

Michelle McGreevey, Golf Product Development Officer, Fáilte Ireland

Paul B. W. Miller, PhD, CPA, Professor of Accounting, Founder and Academic Advisor, PGA Golf Management Program, University of Colorado at Colorado Springs

Ruth Moran, Communications Executive, Tourism Ireland, 345 Park Avenue, New York, NY 10154

Paddy O'Looney, Chief Executive, Southwest Ireland Golf, Ltd. (SWING) Tralee, County Kerry

Mary O'Shea, Advertising & Direct Marketing Executive at Tourism Ireland

David Power, Head PGA Professional, Tralee Golf Club

Pat Ruddy, Owner and operator, The European Club, golf course designer and golf writer, Brittas Bay, County Wicklow

Heidi Sasman, Assistant to John Hehir, Dromoland Castle

Seamus Smith, General Secretary, Golfing Union of Ireland, Maynooth, County Kildare

Ellen Talbot, Executive Assistant to Joe Byrne, Tourism Ireland

Teresa Thompson, Executive Officer, Golf Union of Ireland (Leinster Branch) Maynooth, County Kildare

Mike Touhill, Director of Public Relations, Kiawah Island / Christophe Harbour / Doonbeg

Martin Troy, Assistant General Manager, Jack Quinn's Irish Pub & Restaurant, Colorado Springs, Colorado

Catherine Treacy, Proprietor, Killarney Lodge Guesthouse, Killarney, County Kerry, Ireland

Michael Vaughan, Proprietor, Vaughan Lodge Hotel, Lahinch, County Clare, Ireland

"Anyone can play, but the game always wins"
Tommy Troy

FURTHER READING

Rick Steves' Ireland
You can count on Rick Steves to tell you what you really
need to know when traveling in Ireland

Golfing in Ireland
Rob Armstrong
A comprehensive review of Irish golf courses

Bushmills Irish Pub Guide
Sybil Taylor
A witty and lively guide to almost 300 of Ireland's finest
watering holes. Amazon.com

Irish Pub Songs
Amazon lists numerous Irish drinking and love songbooks
ranging in price from $7 to $20.

Golf Great Britain and Ireland
A traveler's guide to more than 2500 courses in England,
Scotland, Wales, Northern Ireland and the Republic
Ireland

Hotel Secrets from the Travel Director
Peter Greenberg

The Wall Street Journal Guide to Power Travel

Scott McCartney

*"Play Away Please" The Tale of the Sale of Golf's Greatest
Icon-The St Andrews Old Course Starters Box*
John Peter Hagen, sold through **www.playawayplease.
com**

An Amateur's Guide to the Golf Courses of Ireland
Kevin Markam (Collins Press, May 2009).
Kevin traveled around Ireland in a camper van for two years,
playing on and reviewing every 18 hole course he found; all
349 of them.

Plan Ahead and Be Prepared for a Wonderful Irish Experience

NOTES FROM THE AUTHOR

How Golf Has Influenced My Life

E ARLY IN 1996 my good friend Tom Renfrew, PhD, of Drymen, Scotland invited me to join him in a golf-tour business for American golfers. I told Tom that "the offer was intriguing, but I don't play golf." Tom replied that it was then a good time to learn about the greatest game ever conceived. Having spent most of my life engaged in "macho" activities (running, including the Pikes Peak Marathon, biking, swimming, skiing, fitness training activities and hiking), I always thought that I could take up golf any time I was ready. For 14 years, I was Manager of Planning, Design & Development for the Colorado Springs Park, Recreation, & Cultural Services. Part of my responsibilities there were the landscaping and beautification of two public golf courses. One of them, century-old Patty Jewett Municipal Golf Course, is a jewel in the heart of the city. Every time I went there, I marveled at its beauty and while watching the golfers, I would think, "That looks easy enough. I'll try it someday."

Quality Golf International (QGI)

After some thought, I decided that it was a good time to start and I could combine it with the new business venture. I told Tom I was excited about his offer. We created Quality Golf International (QGI) and began a decade of organizing golf tours to Scotland and Ireland. Looking back, joining Tom in the venture and learning the game was a good decision, even though at the time, I didn't know a "birdie" from an "eagle," other than they both had wings and could fly.

The following spring, I bought some books about golf, a new set of custom clubs, signed up for lessons and, in September went to Scotland on my first golf adventure. I took five-dozen golf balls with me and lost every one of them during my 'get-acquainted-with-Scotland golf tour.' Obviously, I didn't impress anyone with my prowess, and I'm sure at that point, Tom regretted asking me to join him, but I was very quickly taken with the whole Scottish golf experience. I love Scotland, not only as the home of golf, but also because the people and the beauty of the country itself make it a must see destination to add to your "Bucket List".

Golf has opened an entire new dimension of life for me. How many golfers get their introduction to the sport by assisting life-long players secure tee times on The Old Course in St Andrews? During the time we operated Quality Golf International, I realized golf is much more than a game—*it is a way of life for many people.*

Although my swing has improved over the years, its beauty never was a factor during the time we organized golf tours through QGI. None of our clients every inquired about my handicap or my golf experience—they were mainly interested in getting that coveted tee-time on The Old Course. Once I realized this, the intimidation that I felt when talking with experienced golfers disappeared and planning trips for them became very enjoyable.

Being physically fit has been a positive factor in compensating for my late start with the game. I can now play a reasonably good round of golf, but equally important to the pure enjoyment of playing golf, the venture led to new experiences and many new friends—around the USA, in Scotland and in Ireland. And I learned that, wherever one travels, no matter if you're waiting in an airport or standing in line for a ticket or a movie, there is always someone to talk with about golf.

USS Abraham Lincoln CVN 72

For me, golf has led directly to other exciting ventures that otherwise would never occurred. For example, in 2005 I embarked on the aircraft carrier USS Abraham Lincoln. During my 24-hour stay, I experienced the thrills of both a catapult launch and an arrested landing, not to mention the flight itself! This excitement was the result of my asking Chuck Zangus, brother-in-law to Tom Renfrew and the third partner in QGI, if I could come out to San Diego and get on board an aircraft carrier that might be docked for maintenance. At that time, Chuck was the Western Region Director for Northrup Grumman and had business associates in the US Navy fleet headquarters in San Diego. Chuck replied to my request with: "We can do better than that," and nine months later I went to San Diego, boarded a COD C-2 and took off for the greatest adventure of my life.

UCCS PGA Golf Management Program

I also played a role as an advisor in establishing the PGA Golf Management Program at the University of Colorado,

Colorado Springs. My good friend, Dr. Paul Miller, PhD, CPA, Professor of Accounting and author of 15 books on accounting, invited me to join the advisory board along with some well-known golfers to offer advice on forming a new PGA-accredited Professional Golf Management program at UCCS. Now, just eight years later, the program is one of the top such programs in the country, thanks largely to Paul but with kudos to many others as well. This was another great experience for someone who knew little about the sport, but I was still able to make a contribution and be among some great golfers. Paul is a lifelong golfer who has played in Scotland several times, but, best of all, Paul agreed to edit the revised edition of the second edition of my first book (see below) and write a foreword to it. I am extremely grateful to Paul for offering his expertise in writing and editing. His love of the game and fondness for playing golf are now reflected in that book.

The American Golfer's Guide To Scotland

Then, we published *The American Golfer's Guide To Scotland*, which eliminated the need to prepare individual travel packets for each tour group as we'd done when QGI began operating. It's fun to search Amazon or Barnes & Noble for our book and see it pop up. I'm honored and humbled to have a copy of that guidebook in the library of the Royal & Ancient Golf Club in St Andrews.

The Old Course Starter's Box (Circa 1924-2001)

Still another adventure in golf opened for me as I updated *The American Golfer's Guide to Scotland*. While researching for the first edition in 2004, Robin Dugmore, Director of

Sales for The Old Course Experience in St Andrews at the time, told me an American was the successful bidder for The Old Course Starter's Box that had been in place adjacent to the Royal & Ancient since 1924. At an auction in St Andrews, on September 10, 2001, John P. Hagen was the high bidder at £59,000. After the auction, he had the box dismantled and shipped to California to be reconstructed on a new private residential golf course development in La Quinta. I followed up with Dugmore's information, contacted John and included a brief summary of this event in the first edition of the Scotland guidebook. But, that is only a small part of the intrigue of the sale, dismantling and emotional departure of this famous icon from St Andrews, as I was later to discover.

In the process of updating the book, I tracked down John to get an update on the status of the box. Calvin Coolidge once said, "Persistence and determination alone are omnipotent," and that is what it took to find him. Eventually, John learned I was trying to reach him and he contacted me with the kind words that he was impressed with my dogged pursuit. During our conversation, John gave me the update on the status of The Old Course Starter's Box that I incorporated in the second edition of *The American Golfer's Guide To Scotland.*

Among other things, he told me he had written a novel about his purchase, entitled '*Play Away, Please' The Tale of the Sale of Golf's Greatest Icon-The St Andrews Old Course Starter's Box,* **www.playawayplease.com**, published in 2010 by Mainstream Publishing and asked me if I would review and comment on the then unpublished manuscript. I agreed and John sent me the text for this fascinating story that was published in 2010 in the USA and the UK by Mainstream Publishing, an imprint of the Random House Group. Every golfer who has been to St Andrews and every golfer who aspires to play the Old Course should read this book. I'm sure anyone who has ever picked up a golf club will enjoy the story.

For me, this developing relationship is another fascinating link in the chain of incredible events that have occurred in my life since I told Tom Renfrew that I would join him in the golf business. This sure has been fun and who knows what lies ahead for me in the world of golf, as I venture further into it on the Emerald Island of Ireland.

The American Golfer's Guide To Ireland

How did this book come about? Having thoroughly enjoyed publishing *The American Golfer's Guide to Scotland,* and missing the international business of organizing golf tours after we closed QGI, I decided to write *The American Golfer's Guide to Ireland* primarily as a labor of my love of golf. (We closed QGI in 2006, over concerns of not having control of air travel for our clients, credit card company compliance demands and increasing insurance costs).

Since I knew very little about playing golf in Ireland, I began planning a research trip. My wife and I made the journey as guests of Paddy O'Looney, who, through SWING (Southwest Ireland Golf Limited), has worked closely with tour operators and individual golfers in Ireland since 1986. I'd become acquainted earlier with Paddy, SWING's Chief Executive Officer, while booking tours to Ireland through QGI.

Paddy arranged a very memorable get-to-know-Ireland trip for us that included golf at the Tralee Golf Club and the Waterville Links Golf Club. We stayed in several charming lodge guesthouses, the beautiful Ballygarry House in Tralee and were guests in the honeymoon suite at Dromoland Castle.

Knowing I couldn't begin to advise you on how to play golf in Ireland, I went on a search to find a life-long Irish golfer who could write clearly about that topic from an Irish perspective. I was fortunate to find Brian Keogh, a well-known golf writer from Dublin who covers professional golf throughout the world. Brian, who is also an accomplished golfer, agreed to contribute his professional writing skills and experience to this project. The possibility for another successful guide increased when Paul Miller agreed to edit the guide, as he'd precisely edited the revised edition of my Scotland guide.

With Brian writing a key segment of this new book, and Paul doing the editing, another exciting chapter of my great adventure into the world of golf has unfolded. Further, I know this guide will be helpful to golfers preparing for memorable tours. With my QGI experience, Brian's Irish golfing and native expertise, and with **Tourism Ireland's** extensive support and input, you may be certain of good advice while planning your golf adventures to the island.

Golf—A Way of Life

Realizing how golf has influenced my life, it occurred to me that others must have golf stories of events that have influenced their lives or generated life long memories. For example, read the story in Chapter VIII of the American golfer from Colorado Springs who scored a hole-in-one at Waterville in 2002 and hasn't stopped recounting the tale. As a result, I've started a column, *Golf—A Way of Life* relating golfers' stories of how golf has influenced their lives, with the intent to publish these tales collectively in another book.

Thank you for buying this book, and if you have questions or have a story to tell about how golf has influenced your life, please contact me at *bill@americangolfersguides.com*. I would also appreciate your comments about this book, especially after using it to plan your trip to the island of Ireland.

Bill Ruskin

"The only time my prayers are not answered is on the golf course."
Reverend Billy Graham

ABOUT THE AUTHOR

Author Bill Ruskin at Dromoland Castle.

Photo Credit: Bill Ruskin

*B*ILL RUSKIN HAS traveled to Scotland and Ireland and was a co-founder of Quality Golf International. In addition to being a fitness buff with a keen interest in the golf business, he has also written *The American Golfer's Guide to Scotland.* Bill pens a column, Golf—A Way of Life. He lives in Colorado Springs with his wife Brigette, and Kepler, a Golden Retriever. They spend as much time as possible outdoors hiking and skiing at Ullr's Rest, their Breckenridge mountain retreat in the Colorado Rockies.

Brian Keogh has been a sports writer for more than 25 years and a full time golf correspondent since 2000.

He writes mainly for the *Irish Sun* but is also a regular contributor to golf coverage in *The Irish Times*, *The Irish Independent*, RTE Radio, *The Irish Examiner*, *GolfWorld*, *The Sunday Times* and *The Irish Daily Star* amongst others. He co-authored Padraig Harrington's book *Journey to the Open* (2007) with several Irish golf writers as well as *Out of Bent and Sand*, the Centenary History of Laytown and Bettystown Golf Club (2009). Brian was elected Chairman of the Irish Golf Writers' Association (I.G.W.A.) in 2011. He lives in Dublin with his wife and son.